Acupressure
For Bodyworkers and Herbalists

Janet "Wolf" Blevins, LMBT, HHP

www.ppp-publishing.com

Copyright © 2021 Janet "Wolf" Blevins, LMBT, HHP

All rights reserved.

No part of this publication may be reproduced, distributed, or transmitted in any form or by any means, including photocopying, recording, or other electronic or mechanical methods, without the prior written permission of the publisher, except in the case of brief quotations embodied in critical reviews and certain other noncommercial uses permitted by copyright law.

ISBN: 978-1-7361839-9-1

Published by Powerful Potential & Purpose Publishing.
Book and cover design by Allison Chick.
Art work inside: Valentin Popov H.H.P., L.M.B.T., M.A. AKA The Bat Dude.
I miss you, your boy wonder
Photography: Christie Pleasants & Janet "Wolf" Blevins. Back inside cover head shot, Caroline Quincy Comer
Models, Latoya Miles & other students.

Printed in the United States of America.

First printing edition 2021.

This book is dedicated to Rosemary Gladstar

People ebb and flow through one's life journey. Many years ago you steered me off my previous course, altered my direction and expanded my horizons. I am honored to know and learn from you. Thank you for all your wisdom, infectious laughter and always sharing your heart and love of travel. Without you I would not be where I am or have met many wonderful dear friends. And to my Ma, Martha who loved me no matter what and encouraged me always.

Words Of Love

Janet is a true healer. Deeply compassionate, insightful, wise and caring, she has hands of magic that work miracles on the body. Skilled in a number of different healing modalities, Janet helps people remember what it's like to feel good. In a simple, practical and easy to understand manner, this, her first book, offers a comprehensive overview of her work and teachings.
Rosemary Gladstar, Herbalist and Author www.scienceandartofherbalism.com

Janet Blevins is a guided teacher and gifted healer. Her class on Chinese Medicine and the art of cupping was practical, accessible and so helpful. I highly recommend her and her work!
Dr. Maya Shetreat Director and Founder, Terrain Institute
Author of The Dirt
Cure www.drmaya.com

Janet Blevins is an inspired healer with a remarkable understanding of Mother Nature's healing herbs. This book is a must for dedicated healers. Ms. Blevins reminds us that all healing modalities and medicines, inherently, come from The Creator.
Dr. Gwen MacGregor   www.drgwenmacgregor.com

Janet was one of my instructors in massage school. We students used to joke about wanting to be Janet's "Grasshopper", a reference to David Carradine's character in the 1972 TV show Kung Fu. Grasshopper was apprenticed to a Shaolin Master of accomplishment and skill, and learning those skills from his mentor helped the Grasshopper to live his life successfully. Janet's background in Chinese bodywork training and teacher meant we got a great start on being successful massage therapist. I've taken a lot of additional classes in Asian bodywork but nobody has done a better job of showing me how to incorporate Chinese bodywork concepts into relaxation and deep tissue massage done in the west today. I still use those tips and tricks she taught us in school. Thanks JANET!!
Ronda Cranford, LMBT NC#8091
www.crane-river-body-balance.com

Preface

I created this book to go along as a handout/manual for my continuing education workshops. It opens the door to understanding the emotions and acu-points of Chinese Medicine. I think of learning about this beautiful ancient practice as gazing at a bright star in the night sky, to blinking and suddenly realizing there is a whole universe and constellations out there. There is so much more to learn and navigate the journey of learning.

I began my exploration after having a traumatic accident at work. It was massage and acupuncture that helped heal me. After I wanted to go to school to learn these modalities. May you enjoy your beginning exploration in the healing art of acupressure. There are many layers to understanding this complex healing art. I tried to summarize and provide an overview of the surface and I hope you find it helpful and it encourages you to further your studies, Janet.

What Is the Theory Behind Acupressure?

Acupressure is just one of a number of Asian bodywork therapies (ABT) with roots in Classical Chinese Medicine and later in Traditional Chinese medicine (TCM).

Chinese medical theory describes special acupoints, or acupressure points, or Ashi (tender points) that lie along meridians, or channels, in your body. These are the same energy meridians and acupoints as those targeted with acupuncture. It is believed that through these invisible channels flows vital energy -- or a life force called qi (ch'i). It is also believed that these major meridians connect specific organs or networks of organs, organizing a system of communication throughout your body. The meridians begin at your fingertips, connect to your brain, and then connect to an organ associated with a certain meridian.

According to this theory, when one of these meridians is blocked or out of balance, illness can occur. Acupressure and acupuncture are among the types of Chinese Medicine that are thought to help restore balance.

How Does Acupressure Work?

Acupressure practitioners use their fingers, palms, elbows or feet, or special devices to apply pressure to acupoints on the body's meridians. Sometimes, acupressure also involve stretching or acupressure massage, cupping, as well as other methods.

Benefits

There's currently a lack of studies exploring the effectiveness of acupressure. Still, some evidence suggests that wrist acupressure may help relieve pain after a sports injury.

In a 2017 study published in the Clinical Journal of Sports Medicine, for instance, researchers examined the effects of three minutes of acupressure, three minutes of sham acupressure, or no acupressure in athletes who had sustained a sports injury on the same day.

The study concluded that acupressure was effective in reducing pain intensity compared with sham acupressure or no acupressure. There was no change in anxiety.

Acupressure may help ease nausea and vomiting in those with chemotherapy-induced nausea and vomiting, according to a report published in *CA: A Cancer Journal for Clinicians.*

A Typical Acupressure Session

Acupressure is often administered by an acupuncturist or trained bodyworker, with the person receiving the acupressure sitting or lying down on a massage table.

Acupressure can also be self-administered. Acupressure is generally done by using the thumb, finger, or knuckle to apply gentle but firm pressure to a point.

The pressure is often increased for about 30 seconds, held steadily for 30 seconds to two minutes, and then gradually decreased for 30 seconds. It's typically repeated three to five times.

Side Effects and Safety

Acupressure should never be painful. If you experience any pain, tell your therapist immediately. After an acupressure session, some people may feel soreness or bruising at acupressure points. You may also feel temporarily lightheaded.

Pressure should be gentle over fragile or sensitive areas, such as the face.

If you're pregnant, talk to your care provider before trying acupressure. Acupressure typically isn't done on the abdomen or certain points on the leg or lower back during pregnancy.

Acupressure shouldn't be done over open wounds, bruises, varicose veins, or any area that is bruised or swollen.

Table of Contents

QI	13
Yin/Yang	15
5 Elements	19
Cycles	23
12 Meridians	27
Jiao, Tongue & Feet	75
Pulses	79
Command, Alarm & Shu Points	83
Cupping	85
Moxa	90
Gua Sha	93
Finding Points Cun Measurements	95
Herbs And Essences	98

Healing,
Papa would tell me
Is not a science
But the intuitive act
Of wooing nature."
W.H. Auden

QI

Classical and Traditional Chinese Medicine dates back thousands of years. The oldest written medical text, Huang Di Nei Jing Su Wen translates to The Yellow Emperor's Internal Canon is dated 100 B.C. Chinese medicine focuses on the balance of Qi or Chi produced Chee or Ki (kee) in Japanese such as Reiki. Qi is energy, life force or vitality. There are several ways we gather Qi into our bodies. We are only born with so much ancestral or congenital Qi so we want to acquire more as opposed to deleting the Qi we get from our parents at birth. While I was in school in San Diego we would tease each other and say don't mess with my Ancestral Qi man.

Ancestral Qi is composed of Jing (essence) and Yuan Qi (original Qi). Ancestral qi can be conserved but not replenished. Acquired Qi is gathered and obtained such as: food (Gu Qi), air(Kong Qi) or exercise (Zong Qi) such as Qi gong or Tai Chi.

Jing (Essence)

Source:
- Derived from parents, supplemented by Acquired Qi (Gu Qi & Wei Qi).
- Responsible for growth, reproduction and development.
- Stored mainly in the Kidneys.
- Weak Jing in children may lead to slow learning or poor concentration and in the elderly may lead to deafness, osteoporosis or unclear thinking.

Yuan Qi (Original Qi)

Source:
- Derived from Jing.
- Promotes and stimulates functional activities of organs.

Wei Qi (Defensive Qi)
- Helps to protect the body and warms the surface of the body.
- - Regulates body temperature by opening and closing the pores.

Distribution:
- On the surface of the body and within the muscles and skin, but not within the meridians.
- Circulation is dependent on the Lungs.

Wei Qi deficiency can be seen in people who have trouble regulating body temperature or catch colds very easily.

"Scientist and Intellectuals,
Those appearance authorities,
Move expertly on the surface,
Beguiled by how things seem.
The tribe of light seekers works with a different kind of sight.
They leave the shore and head to the deeps."
Rumi

YIN AND YANG

In the beginning there was the void which leads to oneness.

Oneness Duality Struggle for Balance

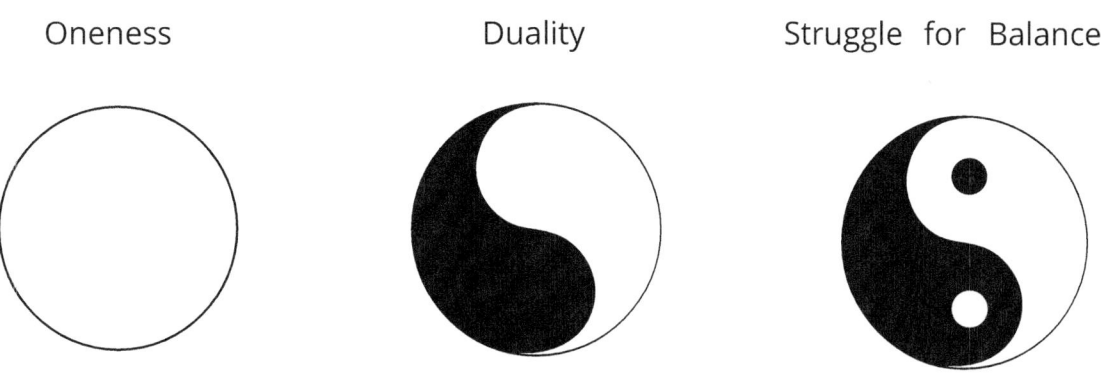

Nothing by itself is either yin or yang; they are a way to express a relationship. They exist in a dance together of never ending movement. Yin cannot exist without yang and yang cannot exist without yin. They are dependent upon one another. Yin is within yang and yang is within yin. Excess yin becomes yang and vice versa. Yin is the substance yang feeds on to gather more yin. They are also in constant motion.

Corresponding Relationships:

Yin	Yang	Yin	Yang
Moon	Sun	Black	White
Night	Day	Obscure	Clear
Solid	Hollow	Retreat	Advance
Female	Male	Grab	Punch
Substance	Function	Pull in	Push out
Right brain	Left brain	Receptive	Penetrating
Condensing	Expanding	Winter	Summer
Intuitive	Analytical	Yielding	Firm
Negative	Positive	Ebb of tide	Flow of tide
Low	High	Waning of moon	Waxing of moon
Inner	Outer	Front & inside of body	Back & outside of body
Passive	Aggressive		
Inhibition	Excitation	Quiet	Loud
Inhalation	Exhalation	Shade	Bright
Entering	Exiting	Lethargic	Energetic
Closing	Opening	Concave	Convex
Gathering	Dispersing	Earth	Heaven
Descending	Ascending	Matter	Energy
Stasis	Activity	Deep	Shallow
Right hand	Left hand	Static	Changing
West	East		
Sunset	Sunrise		

5 Basic Face Shapes

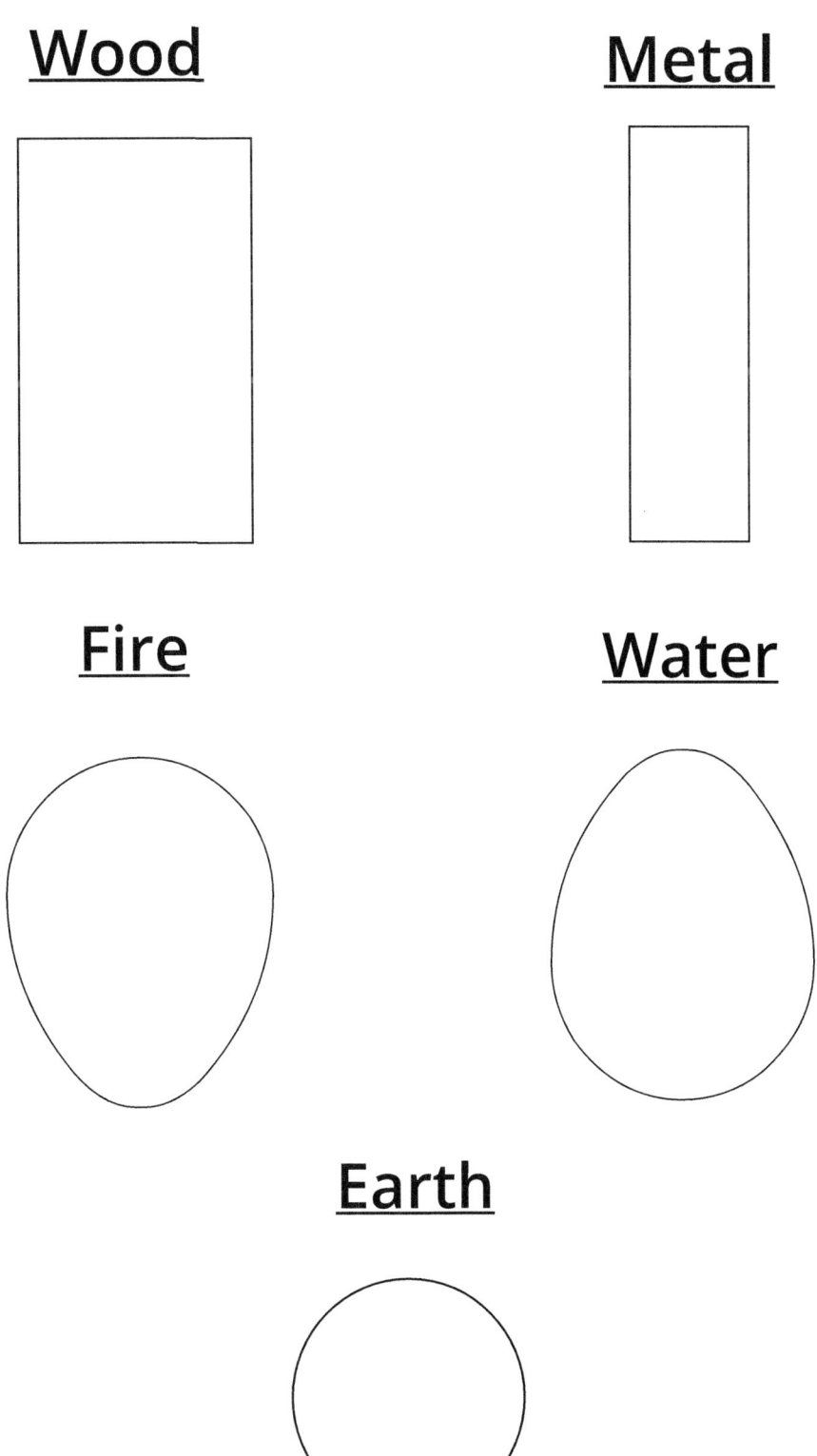

NOTES

"Healing takes courage, and we all have courage, even if we have to dig a little to find it."
Tori Amos

5 ELEMENTS

Water, Wood, Fire, Earth & Metal

Just like the Doshas in Ayurveda, we all have a little of all the Elements in our make-up. One of them will be more prominent, front and center in our characteristics.

Water: *Death & Reassimilation*

Water people want to be apart of and connected but hate contact. They enjoy their solitude but fear abandonment. Water asks "where am I going and where did I come from?" They yearn for the truth but are afraid of what it will mean.

Water wants to dive in but is afraid of drowning.

Water people seek their perfect teacher or direction in life. Water is meant to flow and move. Water fears isolation.

The emotion of Water out of balance is fear.

All phobias grow here when water is out of balance. Balding and hair loss are attributed to this element when it is weak. Trembling and shaking is a natural response to fear. If this condition is constant, one needs to balance this element. Will power and drive are connected to water kidney energy. The voice sound associated with it is groaning. Think of visiting a nursing home and all those folks groaning as they are close to the end stage of life. Or another example, when people groan not wanting to do something, as they are afraid. You scare children or puppies and they pee. Bladder meridian is part of the water element.

Wood: *Birth, Starts, Initiation*

Someone with strong wood is concentrating on goals and how they should start and do them. They wish to be in charge and control things, often being quite pushy. They often miss out on the camaraderie of friends and peers. They make rules but will equally break them all if it suites them, on a dime. Wood is demanding and impatient. They desire freedom but needs to struggle feeling the surge of being unstoppable while secretly fearing loss of control and vulnerability. Sometimes the drive to act is over shadowed by their irrepressible impulsiveness.

Wood people seek the ideal cause or motivation. The emotion of Wood out of balance is anger. The voice association is shouting. Think of people wanting to be heard. Out of balance, migraines and alcohol abuse can fail into this category. Also, if one is not rooted like a tree, dizziness and vertigo can manifest. Any eye problems or spinal(think of tree trunk) look at liver and gall bladder.

Fire: *Growth, Broadening, Fulfillment & Development*

Fire individuals need and desire contact, closeness and intimacy but also crave being alone, solitude. They are terrified of being consumed by the sensations they so long for, yearn and dream of. Fire lives in the moment and says "YES" but fears the future and has difficulty saying "no".

Fire people seek their perfect lover/mate. I call these squirrel people when out of balance. Always starting projects but quickly distracted by another nut never finishing a task. They are running and manic high energy, burning flames brilliant and bright then crashing into severe melancholy. The emotion when out of balance is Joy/Depression.
The Western name is often used is bipolar. The voice association is laughter. If the fire has burnt out, since this element rules circulation, you find issues with varicose veins, cold extremities such as Raynaud's, hemorrhoids, heartburn, hot flashes and lack emotional connection or sexual drive.

Earth: *Centeredness, Grounded and Maturity*

Earth folks love being the center of everything but often feel stuck and weighed down by it all. They want change but fear it. Earth wants to be needed but tend to be immersed and drown losing oneself. These folks give and give; they are the peace makers and listeners. Earth folks always share a smile and deeply care for others. They always remember birthdays and occasions. When they are over extended and always give and never receive Earth elements tend to put on weight to keep folks away.

Earth people seek the ideal family/tribe. The emotion out of balance is worry and over thinking. The voice is sing song, a high pitch up and down. Spleen is an earth element and when out of balance one bites the tongue or inside of cheek. Spleen being the storehouse of blood when weak cannot hold shape so the tongue gets bigger and sits close to the teeth creating teeth mark scalloped edges on it. The little red moles develop, and you can see on the back or chest when massaging. They also have trouble falling and staying asleep. The mind constantly engaged. Pensiveness and over sympathetic are other attributes. Not being connected and grounded, homelessness is attributed to earth out of balance. Earth creates phlegm, think of it as mud when dampness enters. Lipomas, and also what we in the South call back mice in the low back, those little phlegm balls near sacrum. I had an instructor who said when you say a homeless person who was wearing shorts, sandals and t shirt in winter talking to themselves, it was phlegm misting the mind. All that damp heat clouding the thoughts and creating heat. Hot flashes fall into this category of earth out of balance too.

Metal: *Decline & Release*

Metal people want to know who, why and what they are. They seek creativity and invention but hate chaos and disorder. Metal likes to know the outline and order of events. They do not like things to stray off the itinerary. In doing the right thing, they will always play it safe and not go beyond their perceived comfort zone. Metal is distant and aloof but craves relationships. They set high standards for themselves. Metal folks are early and often dress well. These are your A type personalities. In a classroom setting they want a syllabus and get upset if you do not follow it.

Metal people seek their perfect system. When out of balance the emotion is grief and letting go. The voice associated is weeping. The lung is the last thing developed in vitro, so often premature babies develop asthma and allergies. Hoarding falls into metal out of balance, not wanting to let go of anything. Couples married for years, when one dies the other partner often dies within a year of pneumonia. And I also give the example of Christopher Reeve after his tragic accident his wife took such wonderful devoted care of him. After he died she passed of lung cancer.

NOTES

"The wound is the place where the Light enters you."
Rumi

CYCLES

Sheng & KO

These cycles represent relationships, in the body and also in Nature.

Sheng Cycle

Sheng cycle is often referred to as the nurturing, generating or Mother/son, which one element produces the next.

It takes water to grow wood, wood to feed fire, fire becomes ash or earth, earth compresses and becomes metal which liquidifies and produces water.

In a Mother/son relationship, the Mother tonifies the son who then in turn sedates the Mother.

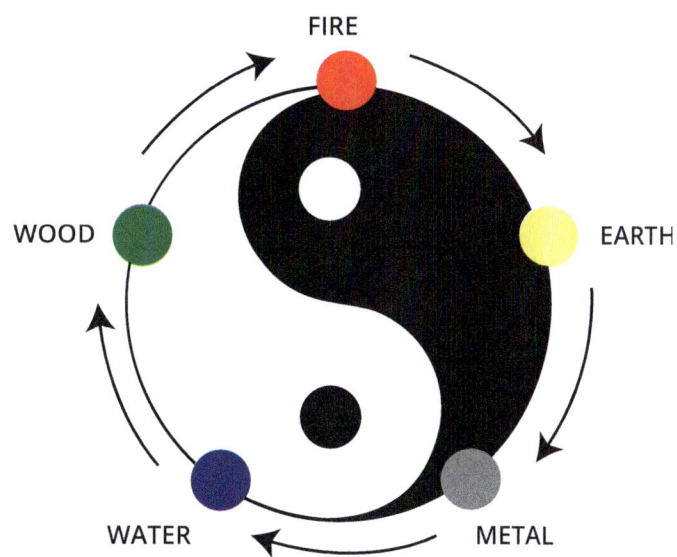

KO CYCLE

The Ko cycle or controlling cycle is often referred to as Grandmother/grandson relationship. It is an inner regulatory action that one element has on another one. Grandmother feels Mother gives too much to her grandson and so she takes away.

It takes water to put out a fire, fire to melt metal, metal to chop wood, wood to cover earth and earth to dry up water.

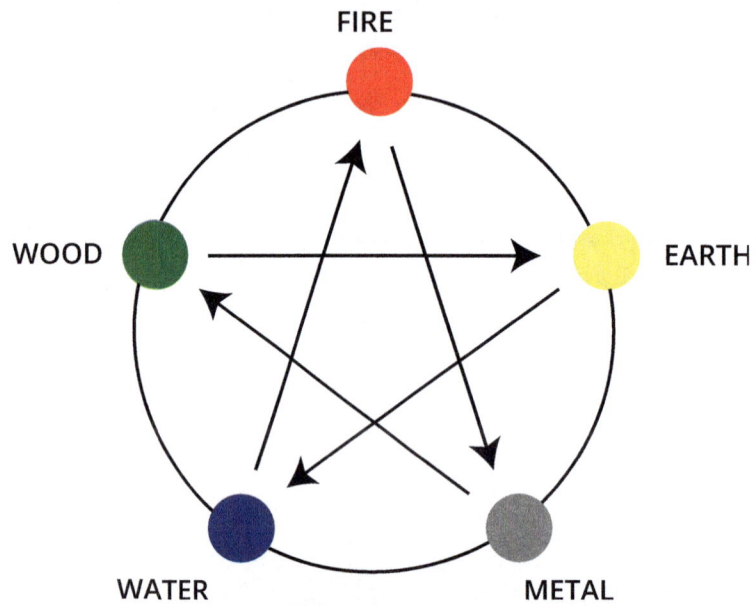

CYCLE OF SEASONS

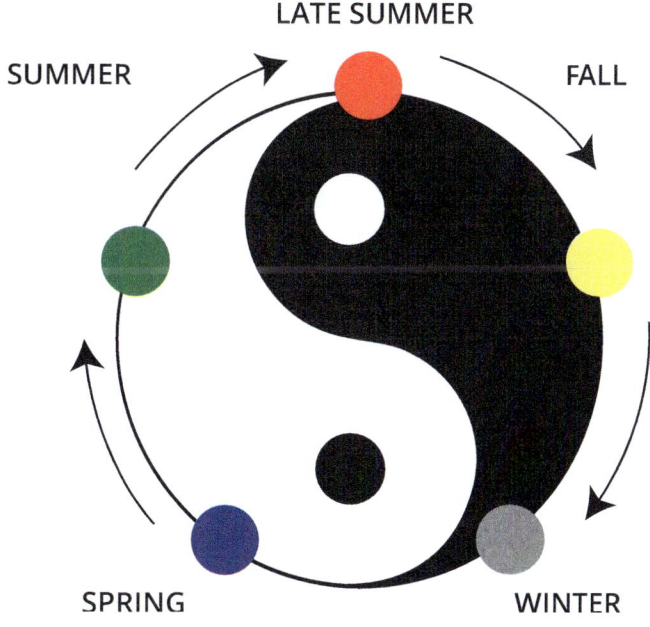

DEVELOPMENT CYCLE

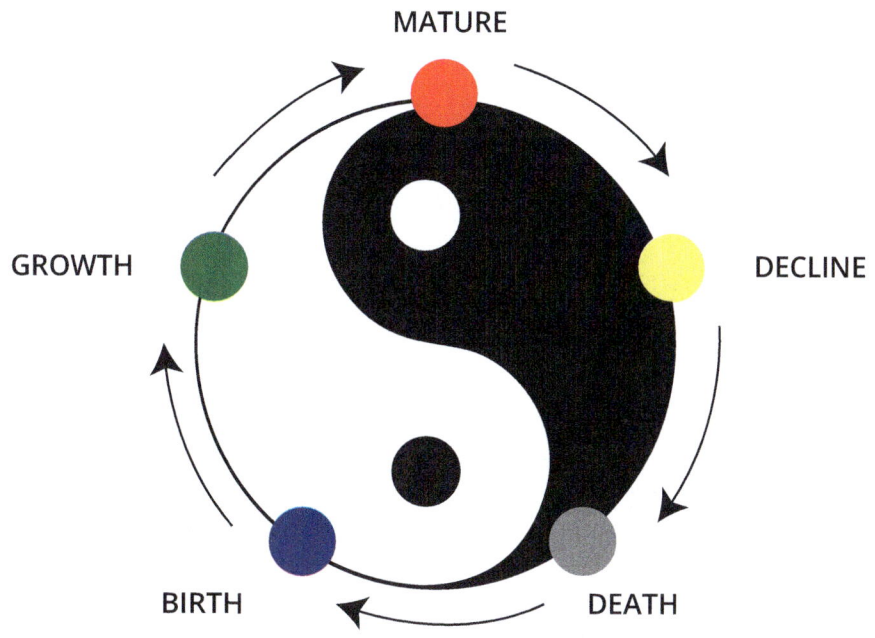

NOTES

"The art of healing comes from nature, not the physician; therefore the physician must start from nature with an open mind."
Paracelsus

12 MERIDIANS/CHANNELS

There are 12 major meridians that run in a circadian cycle throughout the body in a 24 hour rhythm. Each of these is represented by an element and corresponding yin or yang etiology.

I created a type of anagram for my massage students to help them learn the correct order of the meridians in the time cycle. In addition, the way they line up as yin and yang (wife & husband), you can say a wife can stand next to her husband and another woman but not another women's husband. And a husband can stand next to his wife and another man but not the other man's wife. They will flow yin, yang, yang yin, yin, yang and so on.

Luke	Lung	LU	3-5 am	Yin	Metal
Likes	Large Intestine	LI	5-7 am	Yang	Metal
Stories	Stomach	ST	7-9 am	Yang	Earth
Scary	Spleen	SP	9-11 am	Yin	Earth
He	Heart	HT	11-1 pm	Yin	Fire
Sells	Small Intestine	SI	1-3 pm	Yang	Fire
Books	Bladder	BL	3-5 pm	Yang	Water
Keeping	Kidney	KI	5-7 pm	Yin	Water
Profits	Pericardium	PC	7-9 pm	Yin	Fire
Selling To	San Jiao, Triple Warmer, Heater or Burner	SJ	9-11 pm	Yang	Fire
Ghost	Gall Bladder	GB	11-1 am	Yang	Wood
Lovers	Liver	LV	1-3 am	Yin	Wood

	METAL	EARTH	FIRE	WATER	WOOD
Emotions Out of Balance	Grief Letting Go	Worry Over Thinking	Joy Depression	Fear	Anger Indecision
Virtue	Righteousness	Faith	Propriety	Wisdom	Benevolence
Sense	Smell	Taste	Speech	Hearing	sight
Orifice	Nose	Mouth	Tongue	Ears	Eyes
Sound	Crying	Singing	Laughter	Groaning	Shouting
Odor	Rank	Fragrant	Scorched	Rotten	Goatish
Flavor	Pungent	Sweet	Bitter	Salty	Sour
Tissue	Skin/Hair	Flesh	Blood vessels	Bones	Tendons
Secretion	Mucus	Saliva	Sweat	Urine	Tears
Climate	Dry	Damp Humid	Hot	cold	windy
Season	Autumn	Long Summer	Summer	Winter	Spring
Direction	West	Center	South	North	East
Musical note	D	C	G	A	E
Symbolic Animal	Eagle	Bear	Dragon	Monkey	Tiger

All the meridians run in a bi lateral pattern from:
Chest to Hand
Hand to Face
Face to Foot
Foot to Chest
And it repeats 2 more times for all 12 channels.

Example: Lung starts on chest and runs to the thumb then flows into Large Intestine which starts on the index finger and flows to the opposite side of the nose on the face. Lung is yin so it is on the inside surface of body while Large Intestine is yang and flows on the outside surface of the arm.

All yin organs are solid and can be referred to as Zang. All yang organs are hollow and are referred to Fu. Zang handles energy and pure substances while Fu handles impure substances.

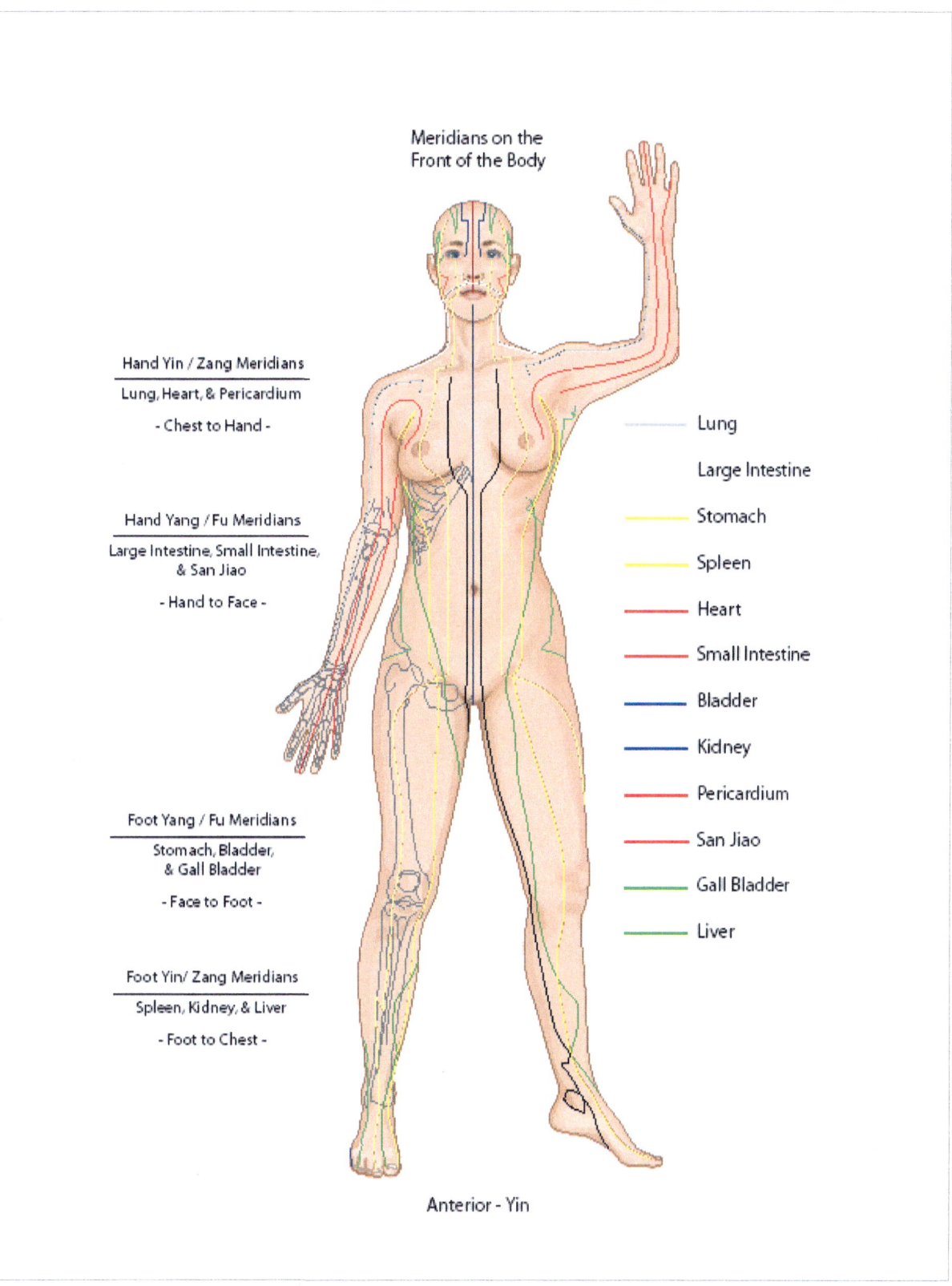

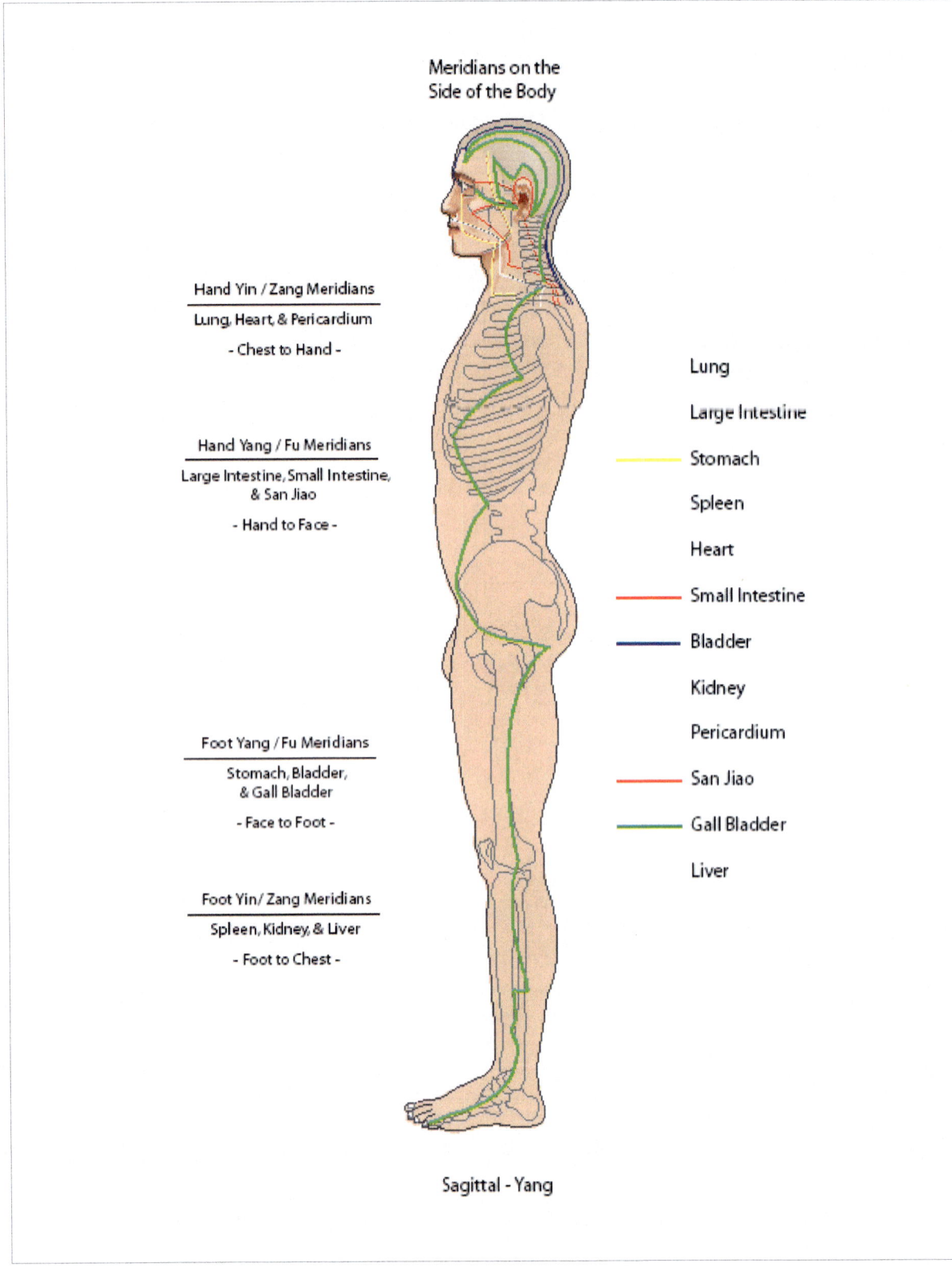

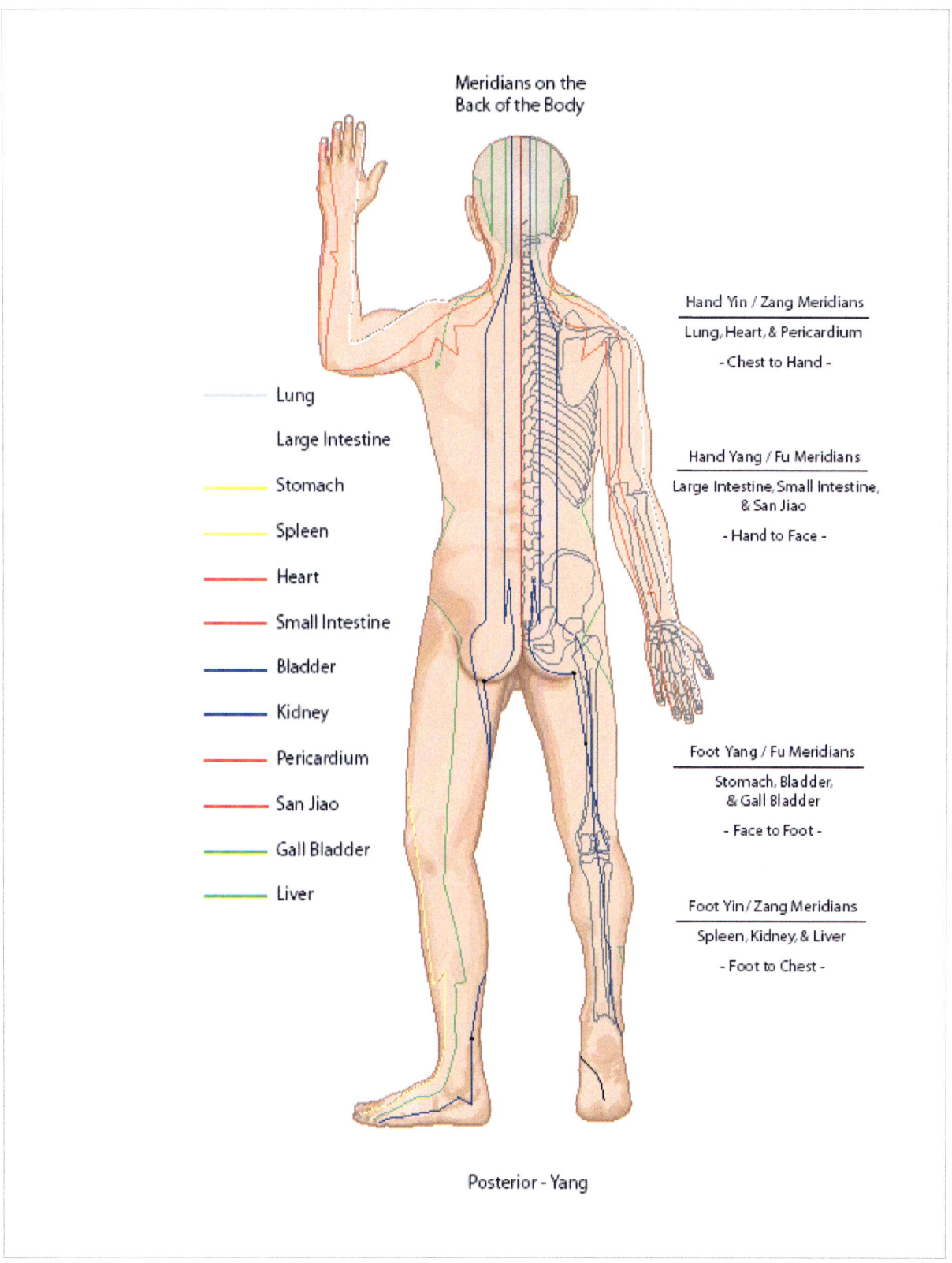

Example: Large Intestine is a Fu organ that eliminates waste and transports partially formed substances. All earthly elements water, wood and earth are 0n the 6 meridians found on the feet with Kidney being the only element touching Mother Earth on the bottom of the foot. The 6 on the hand consist of the 2 metal ones and 4 fire. When meditating and the index finger and thumb are touching, the last 3 fingers relax and are straight out. Those are the 4 fire meridians and it is said you allow your ego to go while in this practice.

POINTS, NAMES AND USES

Note that not all points are used by body workers. Herbalist can use with herbal applications with plants or tinctures. This will be discussed in the herbal chapter later in the book. If using a point for bodywork, almost all points are natural divots, when you find a acupressure point that is tender (ah shi) then use thumb pressure constant static pressure for 15-40 seconds. If the point is excess yang energy use circle motion on point pulling energy out. The opposite is used if yin deficient energy then circle downward spiral.

Lung Points Names and Uses

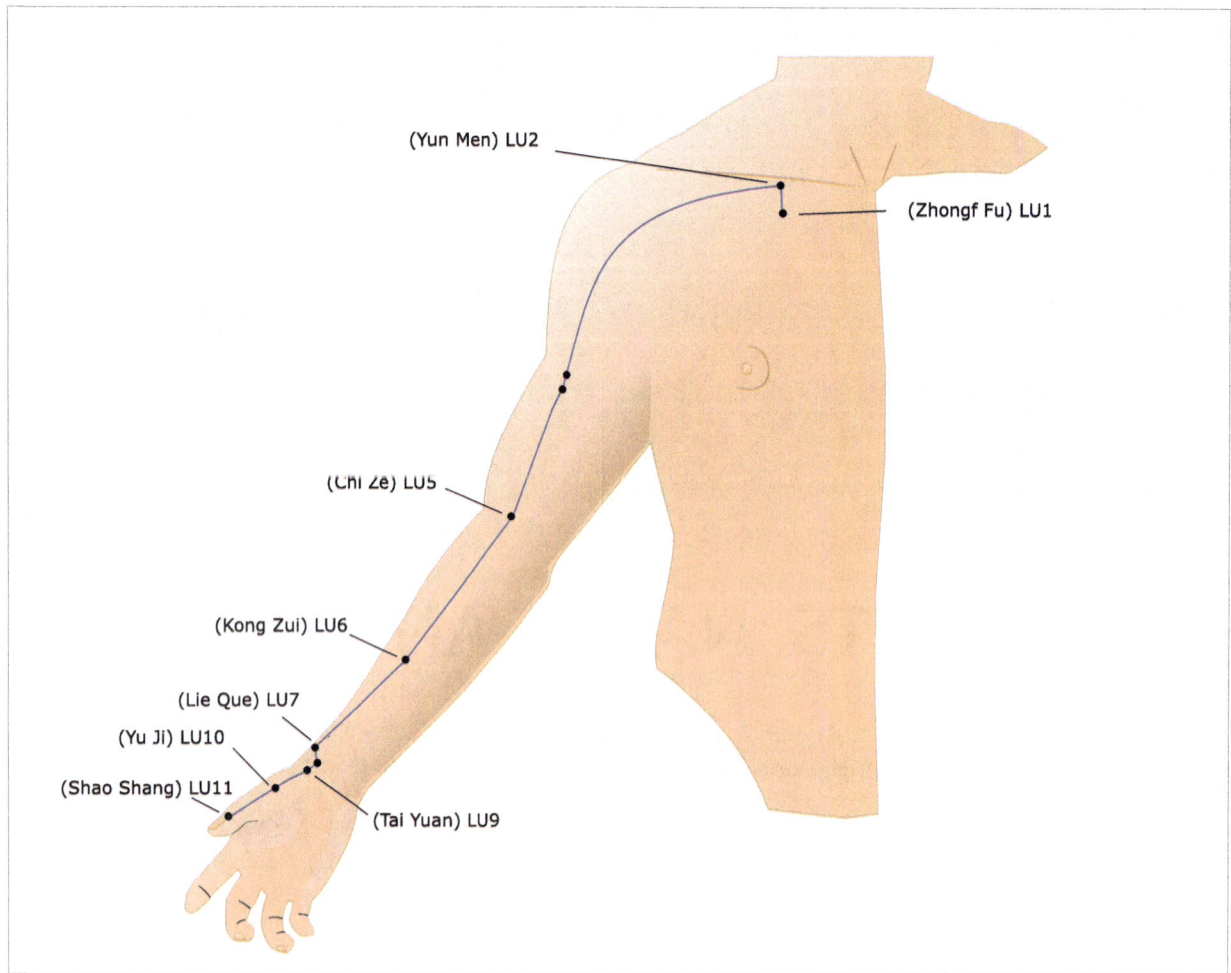

Lung 1: Central Residence, Mansion or Treasury. This point is also the front Mu point for the lungs. Good for pain in chest, coughing and asthma. I also use for grief. Clients presenting with neck and shoulder pain but underlying sadness as shoulders curve towards the heart to protect it. Pectoral muscles shorten and increase pain in neck and scapula region.

Lung 2: Cloud Door or Gate same uses as Lung 1

Lung 3: Heavenly Residence, Mansion or Celestial Storehouse use for Asthma

Lung 4: Standing by White or Pressing white

One of my teachers said 3 & 4 were the widow, breakup or huge surprise loss points and were painful when this accorded.

Lung 5: Foot Marsh

Clears lung heat and expels phlegm. Great for use with athletes at an event to catch breath. Swelling or pain in upper arm.

Lung 6: Biggest or Collection Hole, Supreme Passage

Sore throat, pain in forearm, cough, asthma, bleeding hemorrhoids

Lung 7: Broken Sequence or Divergent Branch

One of the most powerful points on the lung channel, it helps stop persistent coughs. Also uses for toothache and wrist pain.

Lung 8: Channel Ditch

headaches

Lung 9: Great Abyss or Deep Pond

Suffocating feeling and chest pain

Lung 10: Fish Border I tell my students to use when asking for a raise as it helps one find their voice. Also, it is great for sore throats.

Lung 11: Lesser Metal or Merchant

Pharyngeal swelling

Lung

Large Intestine Points Names and Uses

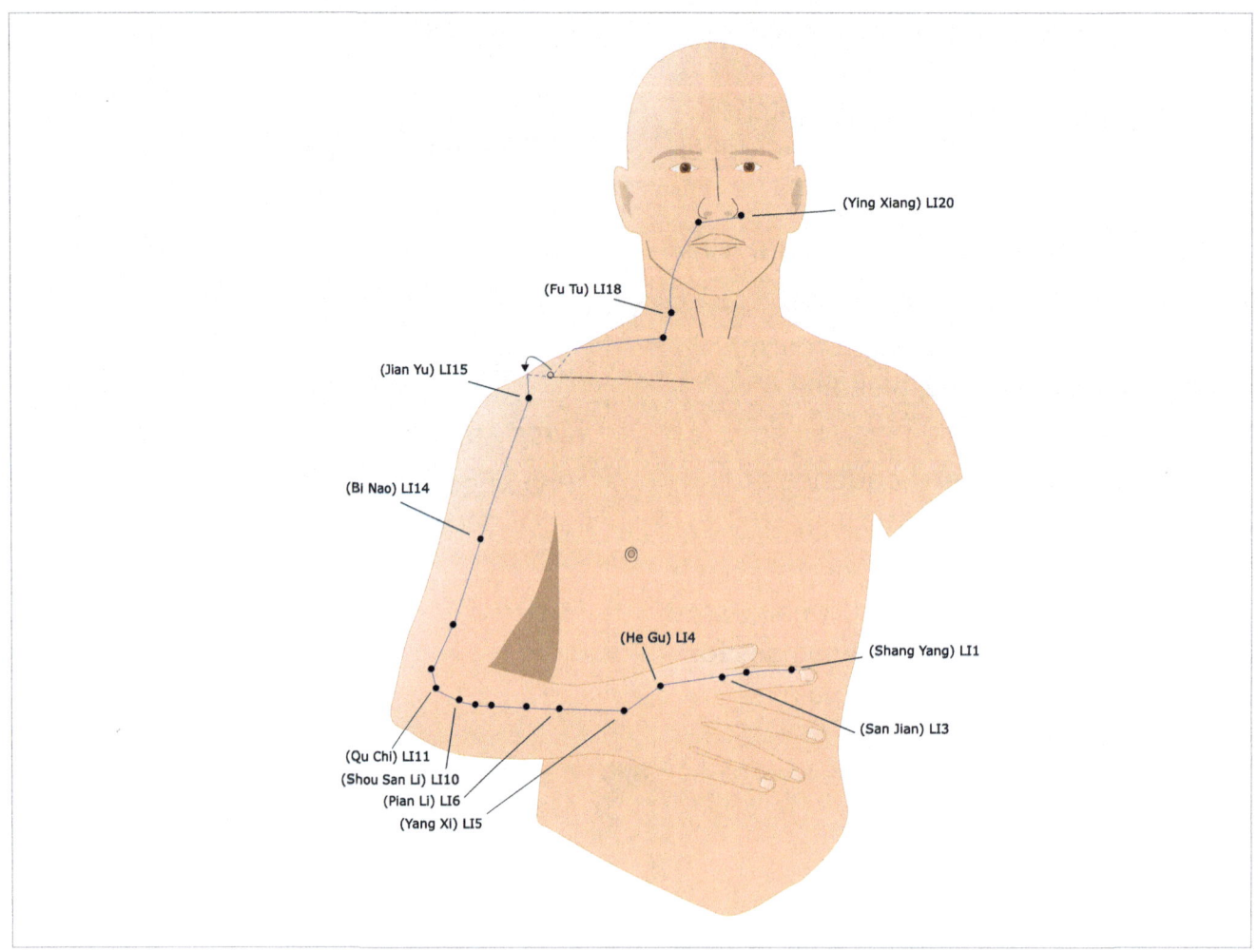

Large Intestine 1: Metal Yang
High fever

Large Intestine 2: Second Space
Toothache, common cold and blocked sinus

Large Intestine 3: Third Space
Toothache and sore throat

Large Intestine 4: Union Valley
Headaches & toothache but *do not use if pregnant*

Large Intestine 5: Yang Ravine
Wrist pain and headaches

Large Intestine 6: Veering Passageway
Pain in forearm

Large Intestine 7: Warm Flow
Abdominal pain & borborygmus

Large Intestine 8: Lower Ridge
Abdominal pain

Large Intestine 9: Upper Ridge
Hand numbness & abdominal pain

Large Intestine 10: Arm Three
Arm and shoulder pain. Frozen shoulder

Large Intestine 11: Pool at Bend
Frozen shoulder

Large Intestine 12: Elbow Bone Hole
Elbow pain

Large Intestine 13: Arm Five
Arm and elbow pain

Large Intestine 14: Upper Arm
Arm and elbow pain. Frozen shoulder

Large Intestine 15: Shoulder Bone
Shoulder joint pain

Large Intestine 16: Great Bone
Arm and shoulder pain

Large Intestine 17: Celestial Tripod
Throat issues

Large Intestine 18: Protuberance Assistant
Throat issues, difficulty swallowing and hoarseness

Large Intestine 19: Grain Bone Hole
Lock jaw

Large Intestine 20: Welcome fragrance
Nasal issues, discharge and obstruction

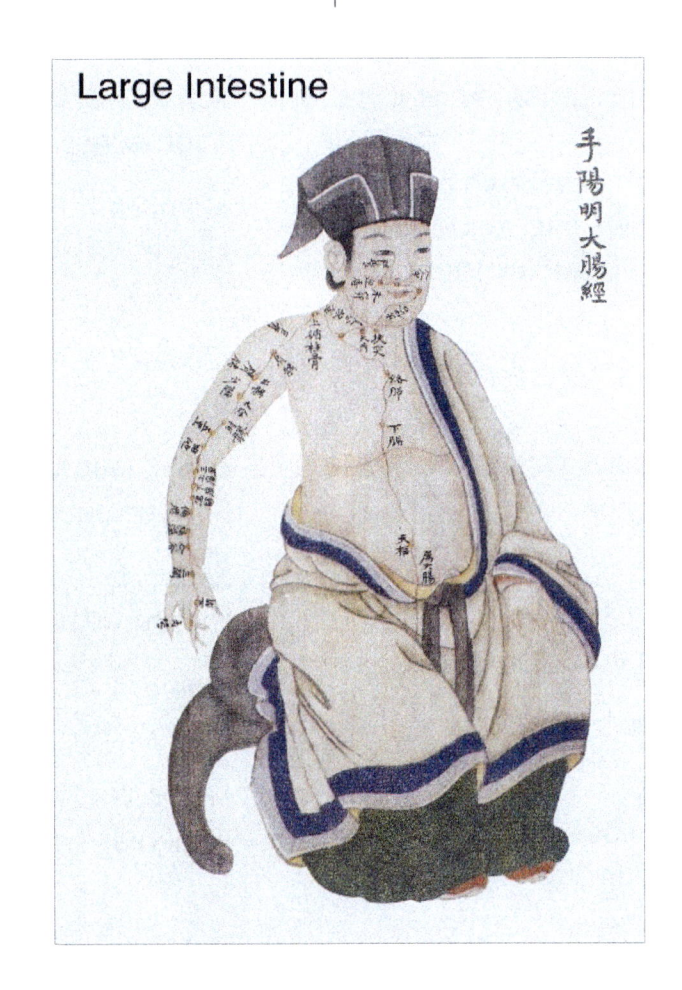

Stomach Points and Uses

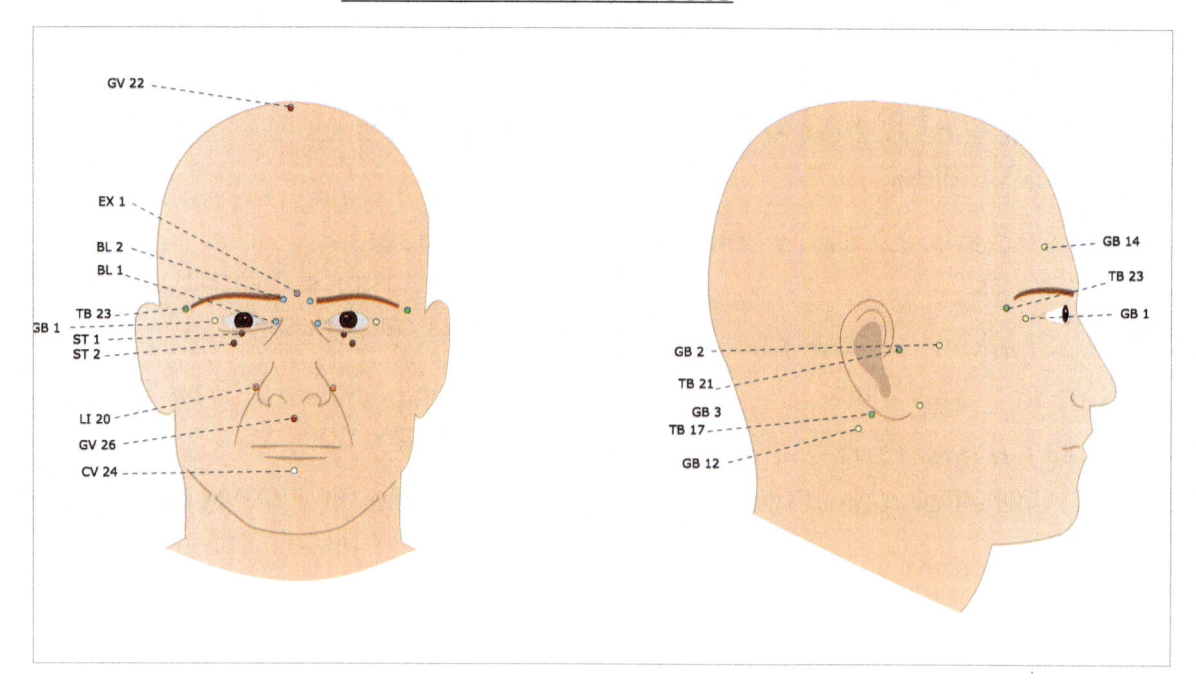

Stomach 1: Tear Container, Holds Tears
Irritations to the eye such as redness and swelling, night blindness and facial muscle twitching.

Stomach 2: Four Whites, All Brightening
Trigeminal neuralgia and facial paralysis

Stomach 3: Great Bone Hole/ Facial Beauty
Same as Stomach 2

Stomach 4: Earth Granary
Same as 2&3 also salivation

Stomach 5: Great Reception, Trigeminal neuralgia

Stomach 6: Jaw Bone or Vehicle, Toothaches

Stomach 7: Below the Joint or Lower Hinge
Toothaches

Stomach 8: Head Corner, Vertigo, headaches and dizziness

Stomach 9: Man's Prognosis or Pulse
Sore throats or hypertension

Stomach 10: Water Prominence, Sore throat, Asthma

Stomach 11: Qi Abode or Residence
Enlarge thyroid sore throat

Stomach 12: Empty Basin or Boken , Cough asthma

Stomach 13: Qi Door, Hiccups, cough or asthma

Stomach 14: Storeroom or StoreHouse, Asthma, cough

Stomach 15: Roof or Housing Fan
Intercostal pain, cough and asthma

Stomach 16: Breast or Chest Window
Mastitis, cough and asthma

Stomach 17: Breast Center
Forbidden point do not use

Stomach 18: Breast Root
Deficient lactation and mastitis

Stomach 19: Not Contained or Container's Limit
Abdominal fullness or pain

Stomach 20: Assuming Fullness
Poor appetite, stomach distention, borborygmus

Stomach 21: Beam Gate, Stomach disorders

Stomach 22: Pass Gate or Closed Door
Stomach distention and pain

Stomach 23: Supreme Unity or Great Yi
Poor appetite and irritability

Stomach 24: Slippery Flesh Gate
Gastrointestinal disorders

Stomach 25: Celestial or Upper Pivot, Diarrhea

Stomach 26: Outer Mound or Outside Tomb
Diarrhea and abdominal pain

Stomach 27: Great Gigantic
Semen emission and lower abdominal distention

Stomach 28: Waterway or Passage
Retention of urine and pelvic inflammation

Stomach 29: Return
Pelvic inflammation, impotence and dysmenorrhea

Stomach 30: Surging Qi or Qi Pouring
Low back pain and irregular menstruation

Stomach 31: Thigh Joint, Anterior thigh issues

Stomach 32: Crouching or Hidden Rabbit, Lower limb issues

Stomach 33: Yin Market or Stagnation
Cold knees, low back pain

Stomach 34: Beam Hill or Hill Ridge, Knee swelling

Stomach 35: Calf's Nose
Knee pain and or swelling or sprain

Stomach 36: Leg Three Li
Vomiting, over indulgence alcohol or food, indigestion, constipation or diarrhea

Stomach 37: Upper Great Hollow or Void, Intestinal disorders

Stomach 38: Ribbon Opening or Narrow Mouth
Calf cramps or spasms

Stomach 39: Lower Great Hollow or Void, Diarrhea

Stomach 40: Bountiful Bulge or Rich & Prosperous
Epilepsy, cough with excessive sputum

Stomach 41: Ravine Divide or Stream
Ankle pain, headaches, dizziness and vertigo

Stomach 42: Surging or Throbbing Yang, Swelling of the face

Stomach 43: Sunken or Sinking Valley
Swelling of the face, foot pain

Stomach 44: Inner Court or Room
Insomnia, thirst, tonsillitis or sore throat

Stomach 45: Severe Mouth or Fundamental Door
Sore throat or feeling of something stuck in throat

Stomach

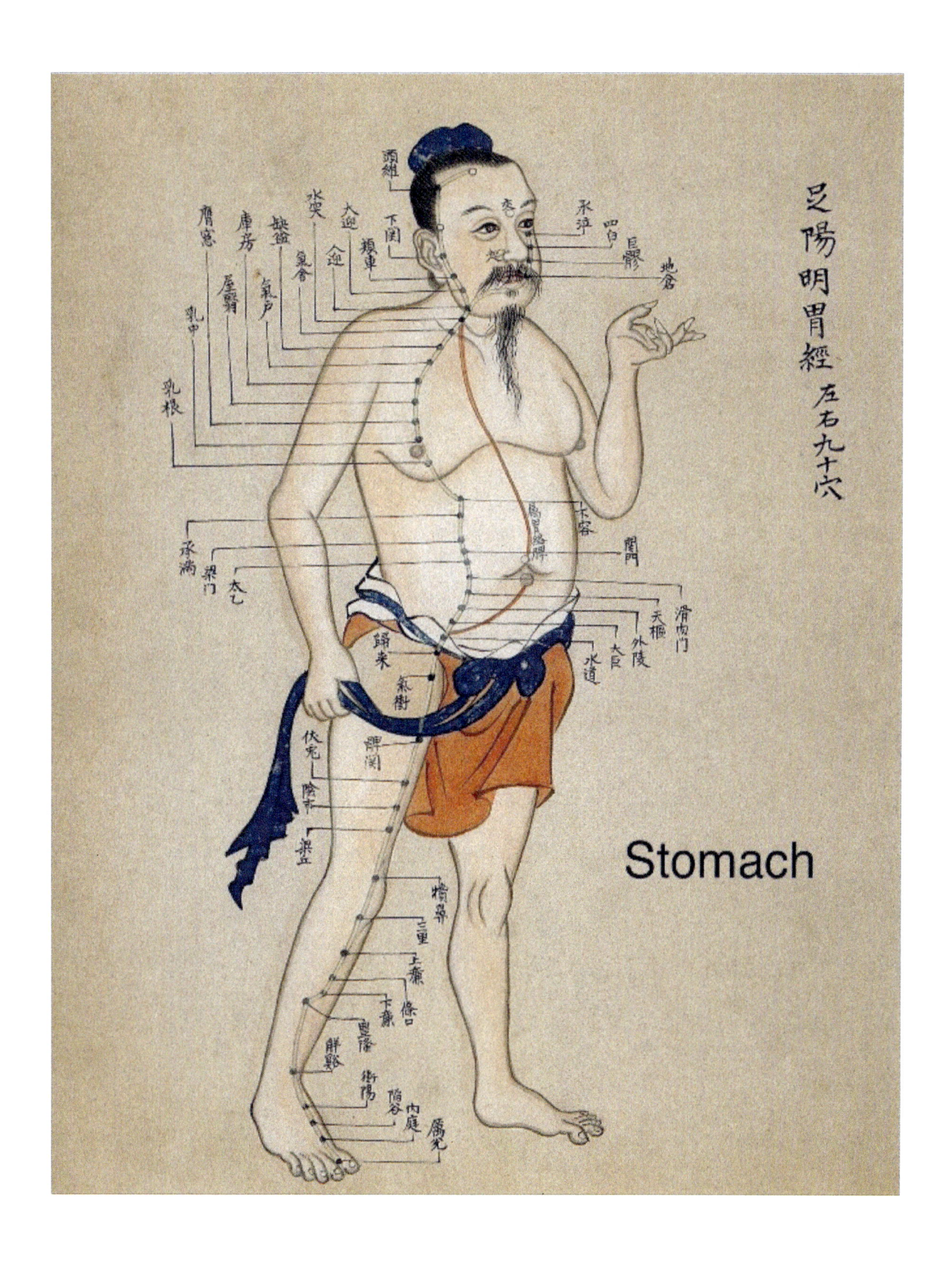

Spleen Points and Uses

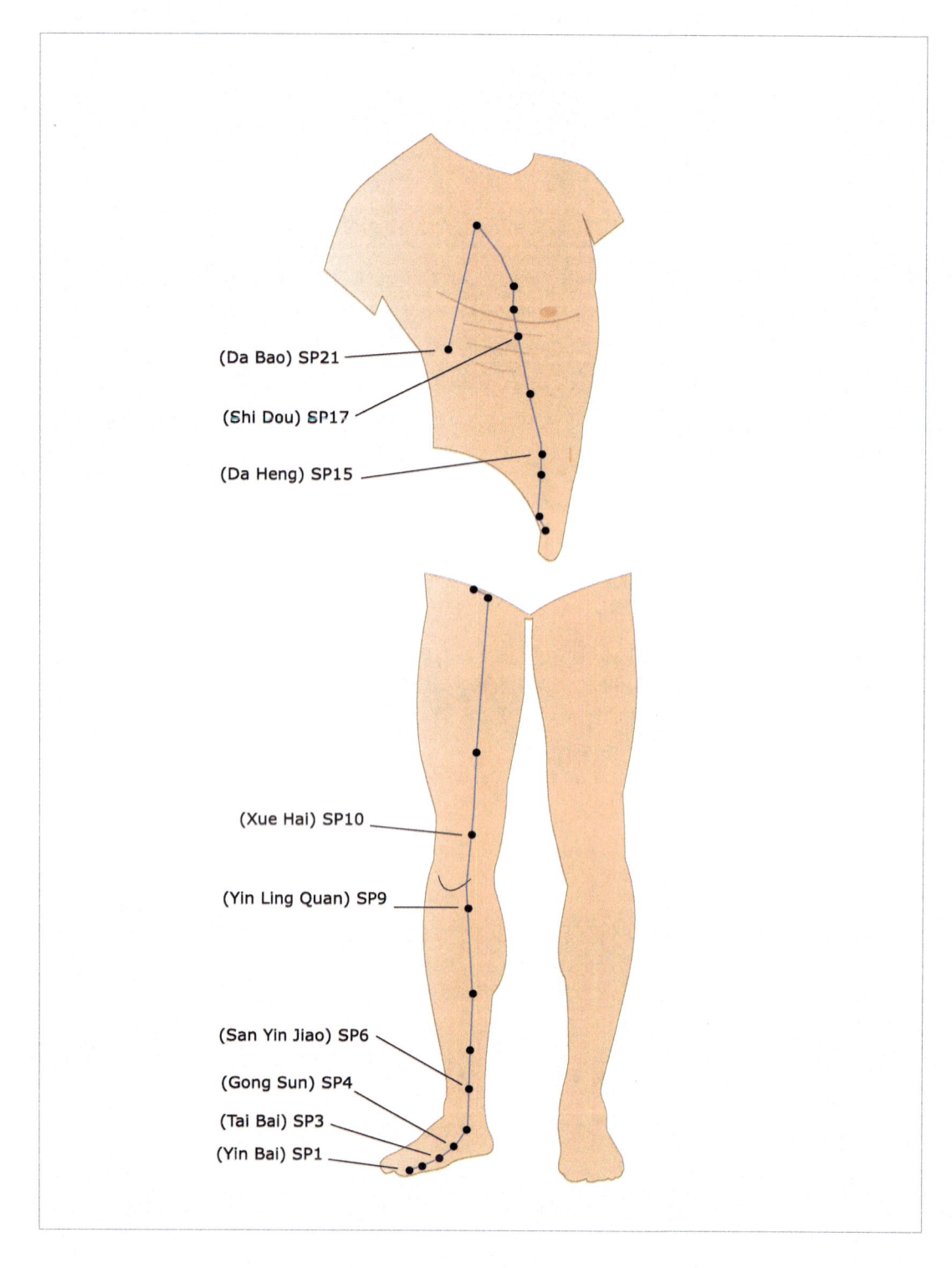

(Da Bao) SP21
(Shi Dou) SP17
(Da Heng) SP15

(Xue Hai) SP10
(Yin Ling Quan) SP9

(San Yin Jiao) SP6
(Gong Sun) SP4
(Tai Bai) SP3
(Yin Bai) SP1

Spleen 1: Hidden White
Nightmares or dream disturbed sleep, uterine bleeding

Spleen 2: Great Metropolis, Indigestion, regurgitation and nausea

Spleen 3: Supreme or Grand White, Stomach pain, diarrhea

Spleen 4: Yellow Emperor or Grandson of Prince
Spleen and stomach weakness, abdominal pains

Spleen 5: Shang or Metal Hill
Jaundice, ankle pain, dream disturbed sleep

Spleen 6: Three Yin Intersection
Disorders or Reproductive and urinary systems as well as digestive

Spleen 7: Leaking Valley
Cold legs and knees, seminal emission, abdominal distention

Spleen 8: Earth's Crux or Change
Irregular menstruation, edema

Spleen 9: Yin Mound Spring, Urinary infections

Spleen 10: Sea of Blood
Great for post partum depression, getting rid of afterbirth after delivery, reproductive disorders and you need blood flow for coitus, excellent for either sex, Eczema, arthritis of knees

Spleen 11: Winnower or Basket Gate, Pain & swelling of inguinal region

Spleen 12: Surging Gate or Pulsating Door
Uterine bleeding and leukorrhea

Spleen 13: Bowel Abode or Converging House
Abdominal masses and pain

Spleen 14: Abdominal Bind or Stasis, Constipation

Spleen 15: Great Horizontal or Great Transverse Line
Constipation/ diarrhea/dysentery

Spleen 16: Abdominal Lament or Cry, Indigestion

Spleen 17: Food Hole or Cavity, Fullness and or pain in chest

Spleen 18: Celestial Ravine or Stream
Same as 17 plus lactation difficulties

Spleen 19: Chest Village or Home, Same as 17

Spleen 20: All Rounding Flourishing or Whole Nourishment
Poor appetite, chest fullness and cough

Spleen 21: Great Embracement or Control
Weakness and pain of whole body, asthma

Spleen

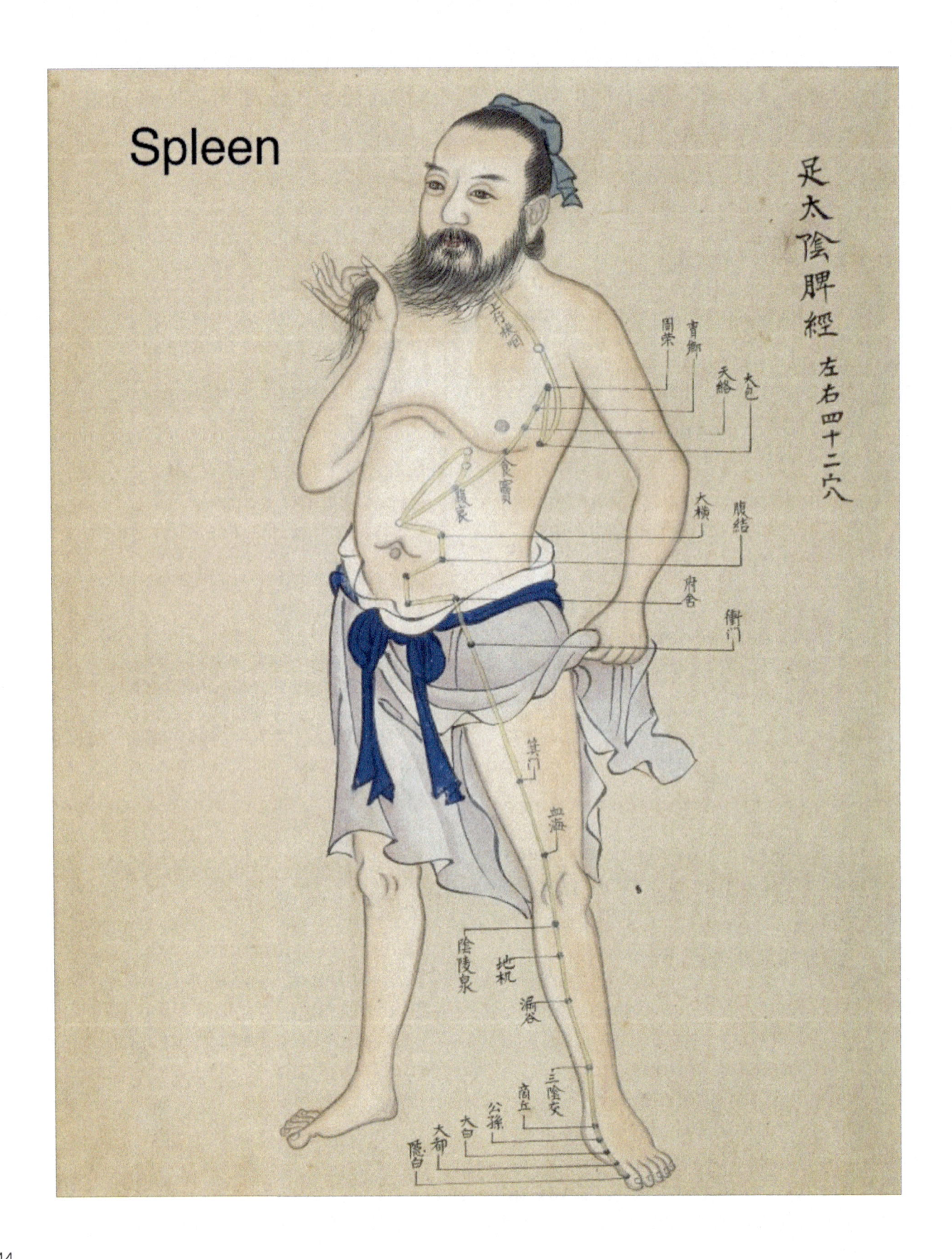

Heart Points and Uses

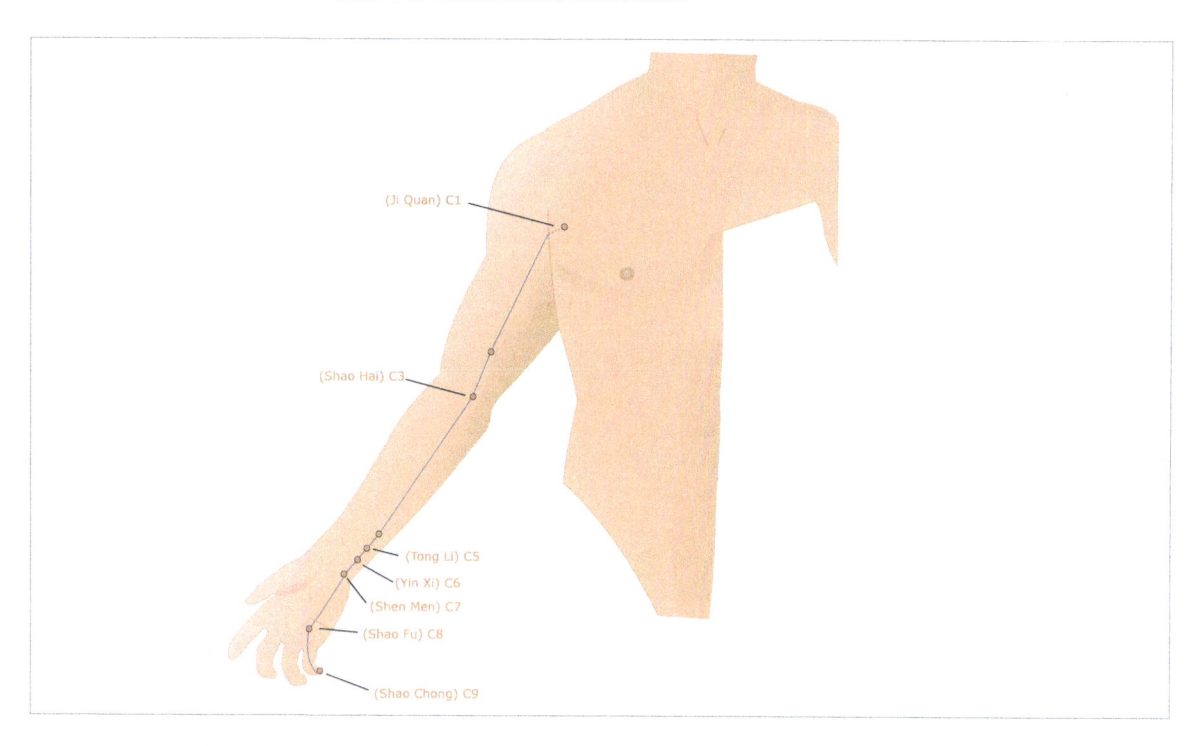

Heart 1: Highest or Running Spring
Dry throat Chest pain.

Heart 2: Cyan Spirit or Green Effect
Shoulder, chest and arm pain

Heart 3: Lesser or Young Sea numbness of arm, pain and swelling in lymph glands in arm pit. Pain in the heart and hand tremors. Mental disorders

Heart 4: Spirit Pathway or Mind Passage elbow issues, mental issues

Heart 5: Connecting Li or Inner Communication
arm & wrist pain, hysteria, hoarseness

Heart 6: Yin Cleft or Crevice chest pain, night sweating

Heart 7: Spirit Gate
insomnia, chest & wrist pain

Heart 8: Lesser or Young Mansion Palpitations, chest pain

Heart 9: Lesser Surge clients in shock, palpitations & chest pain. My instructor once said biting on the nail bed of the little finger where Heart meridian ends at H9 and Small Intestine 1 begins is great for adding a little time if you feel you are having a heart attack after you call 911.

Heart

手少陰心經

Small Intestine Points and Uses

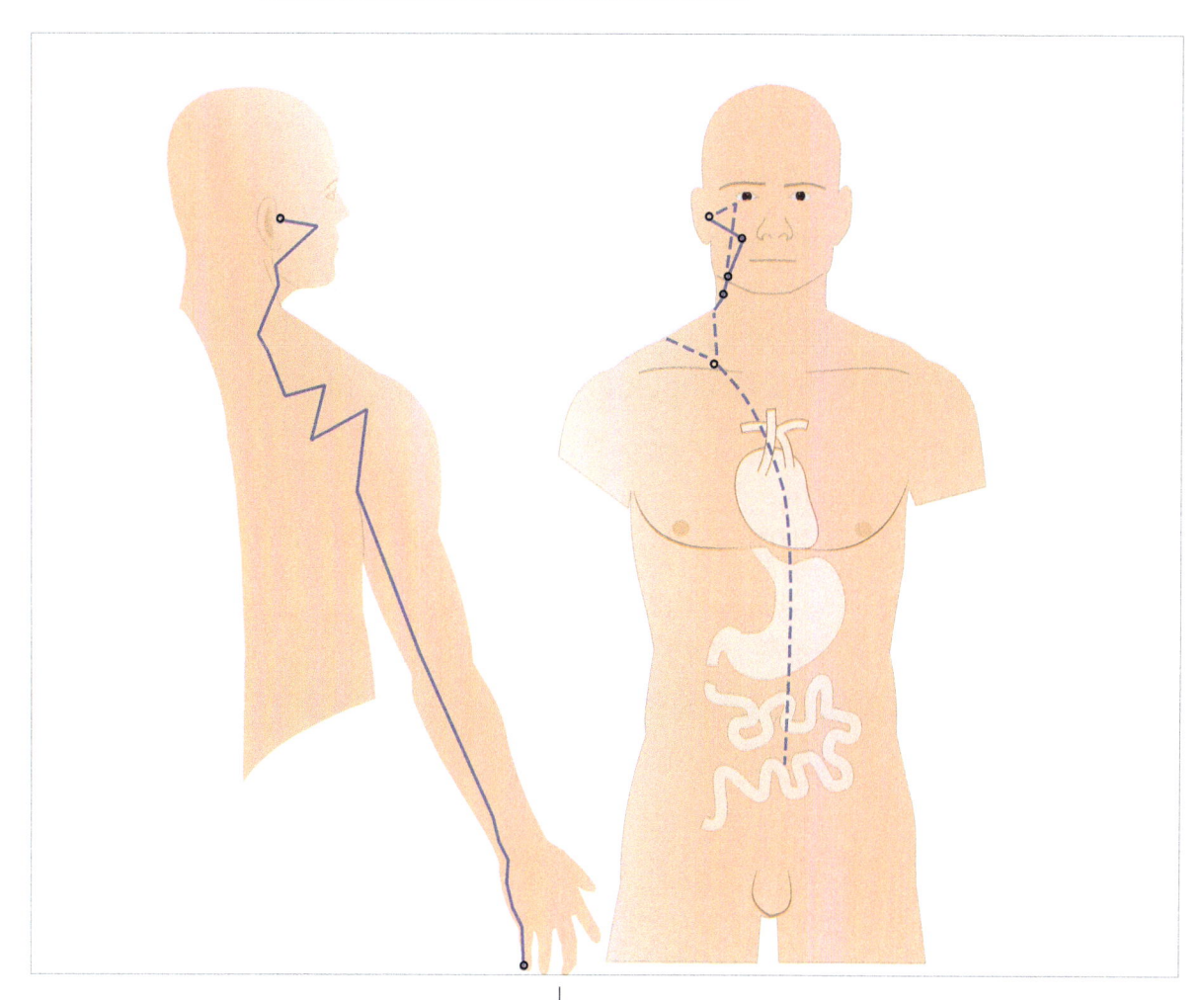

Small Intestine 1: Lesser Marsh or Small Moistening
Mental illness, head, eye ear and throat problems

Small Intestine 2: Front Valley
Lactation difficulties after childbirth, headache and eye pain

Small Intestine 3: Back Ravine or Stream
Twitching of elbow, arms or fingers, neck rigidity

Small Intestine 4: Wrist Bone, Wrist pain

Small Intestine 5: Yang Valley, Deafness, tinnitus, dizziness

Small Intestine 6: Nursing or Benefiting the Aged
Occipital headaches, appendicitis, shoulder and back pain, intercostal neuralgia

Small Intestine 7: Branch to the Correct or Meridian's Branch, Finger, neck and back pain

Small Intestine 8: Small Sea, Ulnar nerve issues, pain neck, shoulder and elbow

Small Intestine 9: True Shoulder, Toothache tinnitus

Small Intestine 10: Upper Arm Shu or Point of Humerus, Frozen shoulder

Small Intestine 11: Celestial Gathering or Heavenly Convergence
Pain in shoulder & arm

Small Intestine 12: Grasping the Wind or Wind Receiver, Shoulder & arm pain

Small Intestine 13: Crooked or Curved Wall, Shoulder & arm pain

Small Intestine 14: Outer Shoulder Shu or Point Shoulder & back pain, neck rigidity

Small Intestine 15: Central Shoulder Shu or Point
Bloody vomiting, back & shoulder pain

Small Intestine 16: Celestial Window, Sore itchy throat, tinnitus

Small Intestine 17: Celestial Countenance or Appearance
Pain, swelling of neck, sore throat

Small Intestine 18: Cheek Bone Hole
Trigeminal neuralgia, facial paralysis, toothache, twitching of eyeballs

Small Intestine 19: Auditory Place or Hearing Palace
Great for vertigo and ear disorders

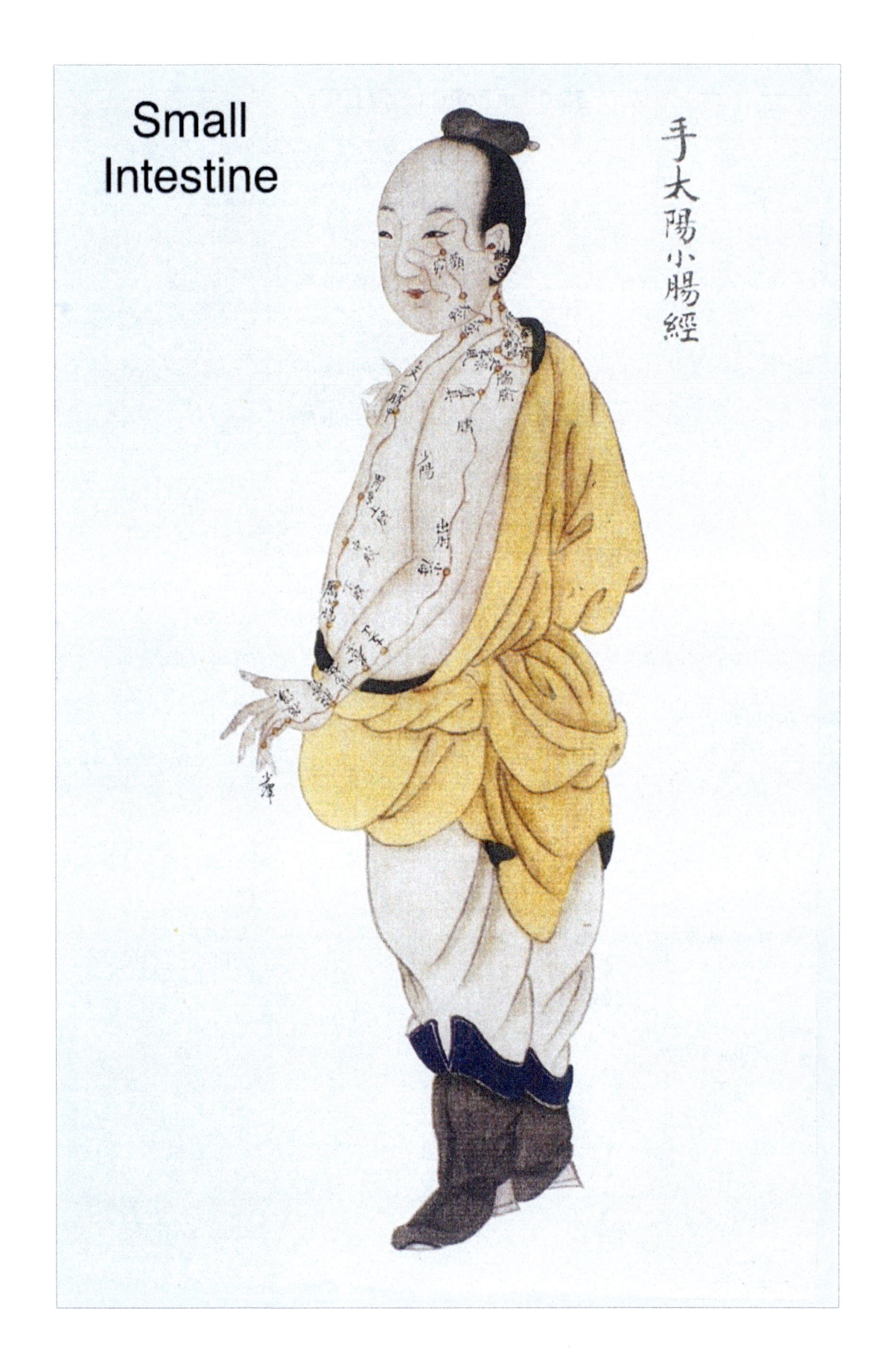

Small Intestine

手太陽小腸經

Bladder Points and Uses

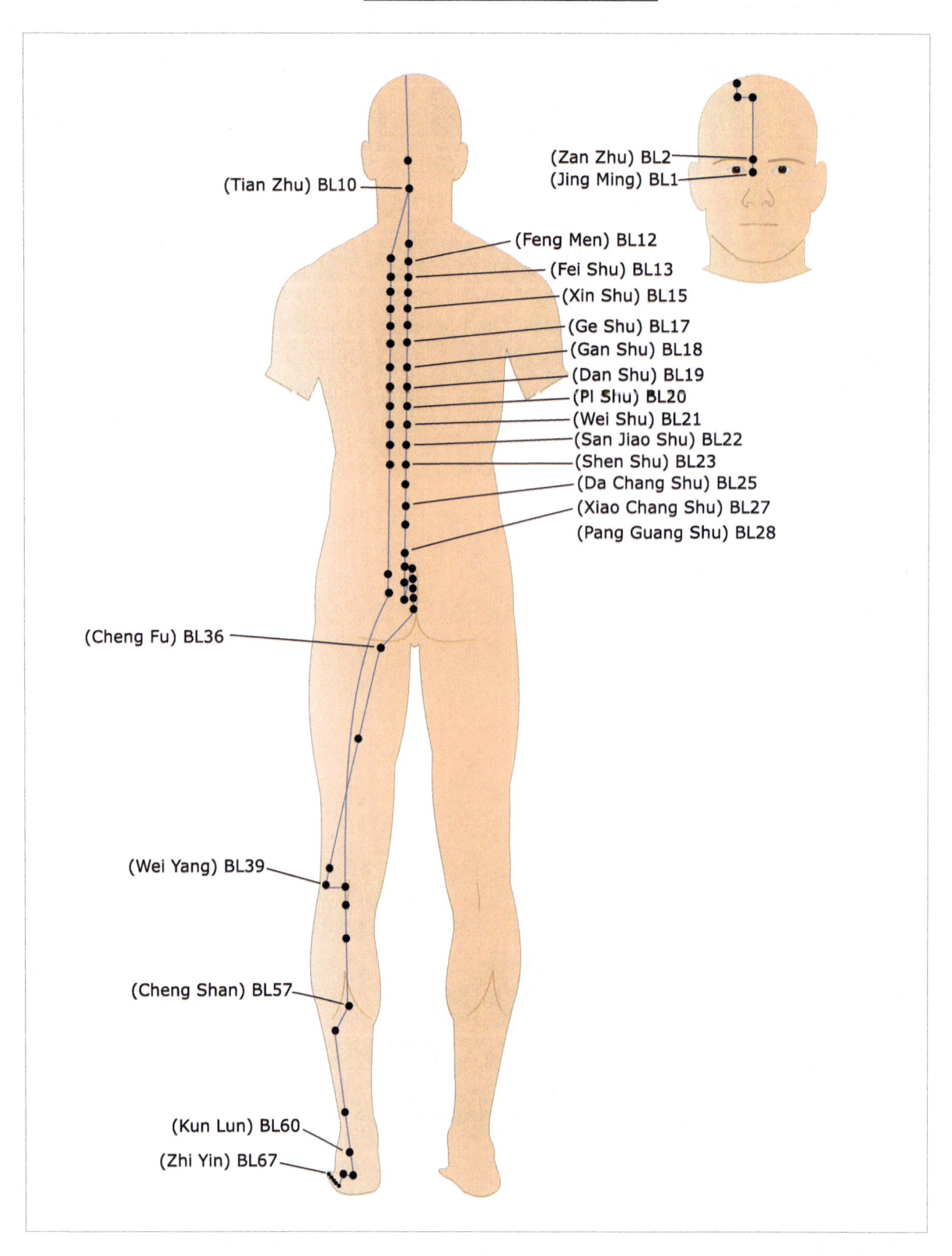

(Tian Zhu) BL10
(Zan Zhu) BL2
(Jing Ming) BL1
(Feng Men) BL12
(Fei Shu) BL13
(Xin Shu) BL15
(Ge Shu) BL17
(Gan Shu) BL18
(Dan Shu) BL19
(Pi Shu) BL20
(Wei Shu) BL21
(San Jiao Shu) BL22
(Shen Shu) BL23
(Da Chang Shu) BL25
(Xiao Chang Shu) BL27
(Pang Guang Shu) BL28
(Cheng Fu) BL36
(Wei Yang) BL39
(Cheng Shan) BL57
(Kun Lun) BL60
(Zhi Yin) BL67

Bladder is the longest meridian in the body starting at the medial corner of the eye where you cry and goes to the wee wee toe.

A little fun saying I use to help my students remember in class

Bladder 1: Bright Eyes
Myopia, visual hallucinations, night blindness, cataract, eye issues

Bladder 2: Bamboo Gathering
Headaches, blurred vision, vertigo

Bladder 3: Eyebrow Ascension or Pouring
Dizziness, epilepsy, headaches

Bladder 4: Deviating or Irregular Turn, Blurred vision

Bladder 5: Fifth Place, Vertigo, dizziness

Bladder 6: Light Guard or Taking light, Headaches, blurred vision

Bladder 7: Celestial Connection or Heaven
Blurred vision, headaches, epilepsy

Bladder 8: Declining Connection or Vessels, Eye pain and redness

Bladder 9: Jade Pillow, Blurred vision, neck and head pain

Bladder 10: Celestial Pillar, Neck and head pain, insomnia

Bladder 11: Great or Big Shutter
Back and neck pain, headaches, cough, fever

Bladder 12: Wind Gate
Back, neck pain, cough, cold with fever

Bladder 13: Lung Shu or Point, Night sweating

Bladder 14: Pericardium Shu or Point
Angina, suffocating sensation

Bladder 15: Heart Shu or Point
Irritability, forgetfulness, palpations, insomnia

Bladder 16: Governor/ Du vessel Shu, Heart pain

Bladder 17: Diaphragm Shu or Point, Cough, asthma

Bladder 18: Liver Shu or Point, Liver & gall bladder disorders, glaucoma, myopia

Bladder 19: Gall Bladder Shu or Point, Same as 18 and bitter taste in mouth

Bladder 20: Spleen Shu or Point, Indigestion, diarrhea, anemia

Bladder 21: Stomach Shu or Point

Weakness of spleen & stomach, pain in chest or abdomen

Bladder 22: San Jiao Shu or Point Loose stool with undigested food, lower back pain

Bladder 23: Kidney Shu or Point, Impotence, irregular menstrual cycle

Bladder 24: Sea of Qi Shu or Point, Hemorrhoid bleeding

Bladder 25: Large Intestine Shu or Point, Lumbago

Bladder 26: Origin Pass Shu or Point, Low back pain

Bladder 27: Small Intestine Shu or Point, Lower abdominal pain

Bladder 28: Bladder Shu or Point, Pin in lumbar sacral region, urine retention

Bladder 29: Central Backbone Shu or Point, Low back pain, stiffness

Bladder 30: White Ring Shu or Point, Hip joint and low back pain

Bladder 31: Upper Bone Hole

Bladder 32: Second Bone Hole

Bladder 33: Central Bone Hole

Bladder 34: Lower Bone Hole, 31-34 reproductive and urinary diseases

Bladder 35: Meeting of the Yang, Diarrhea, hemorrhoids, impotence

Bladder 36: Hold and Support Sciatica, constipation, hemorrhoids. Great for low back pain

Bladder 37: Gate of Abundance or Thick Red Gate, Sciatica, lumbago

Bladder 38: Superficial or Floating Cleft, Numbness in glutes

Bladder 39: Bend Yang, Cramping of foot or legs

Bladder 40: Bend Middle, Sunstroke, calf contractions, sciatica, low back pain

Bladder 41: Attached Branch Shoulder, back & neck pain, numbness of elbow and arm

Bladder 42: Door of the Corporeal Soul or Spirit Shelter
Stops cough and asthma

Bladder 43: Vital Center Shu or Point
Poor memory, cough, tuberculosis, asthma

Bladder 44: Spirit Hall, Calms mind, spirit

Bladder 45: Yi Xi, Shoulder, back pain, cough

Bladder 46: Diaphragm Pass, Hiccups, acid reflux

Bladder 47: Hun or Soul Gate, Liver and mental disorders

Bladder 48: Yang Head Rope, Jaundice, hepatitis

Bladder 49: Reflexion Abode or Emotion's Residence
Poor appetite associated with emotions

Bladder 50: Stomach Granary or Storehouse

Strengthen the spleen and stomach, poor appetite

Bladder 51: Huang or Energy Gate, Constipation, abdominal pain

Bladder 52: Will Chamber or Residence, Edema, lumbago, impotence

Bladder 53: Bladder Huang or Energy, Urinary disorders

Bladder 54: Sequential Limit or Edge
Scrotum swelling, hemorrhoids, motor impairment

Bladder 55: Yang Union, Back pain, uterine bleeding

Bladder 56: Sinew Support, Tendon spasms

Bladder 57: Mountain Support, Anal fissure, prolapse rectum
I use 56 & 57 for plantar fasciitis

Bladder 58: Taking Flight, Back pain, leg weakness

Bladder 59: Instep Yang, Headache

Bladder 60: Kun Lun Mountains
Retention of placenta, blurred vision, stiff neck

Bladder 61: Subservient Visitor or Servant's Worship
Calf contractions, heel pain

Bladder 62: Extending Vessel or Relaxing Meridians

Malposition of fetus, dizziness, blurred vision, pain in lower extremities

Bladder 63: Metal or Golden Gate, Ankle pain, epilepsy, back ache

Bladder 64: Capital or Big Bone, Knee pain, headache

Bladder 65: Bundle Bone or Bone Shu, Mental confusion, headaches

Bladder 66: Valley Passage, Blurred vision, neck rigidity & headaches

Bladder 67: Reaching Yin
Difficult labor. Moxa on this point will turn a breached baby

Bladder Channel

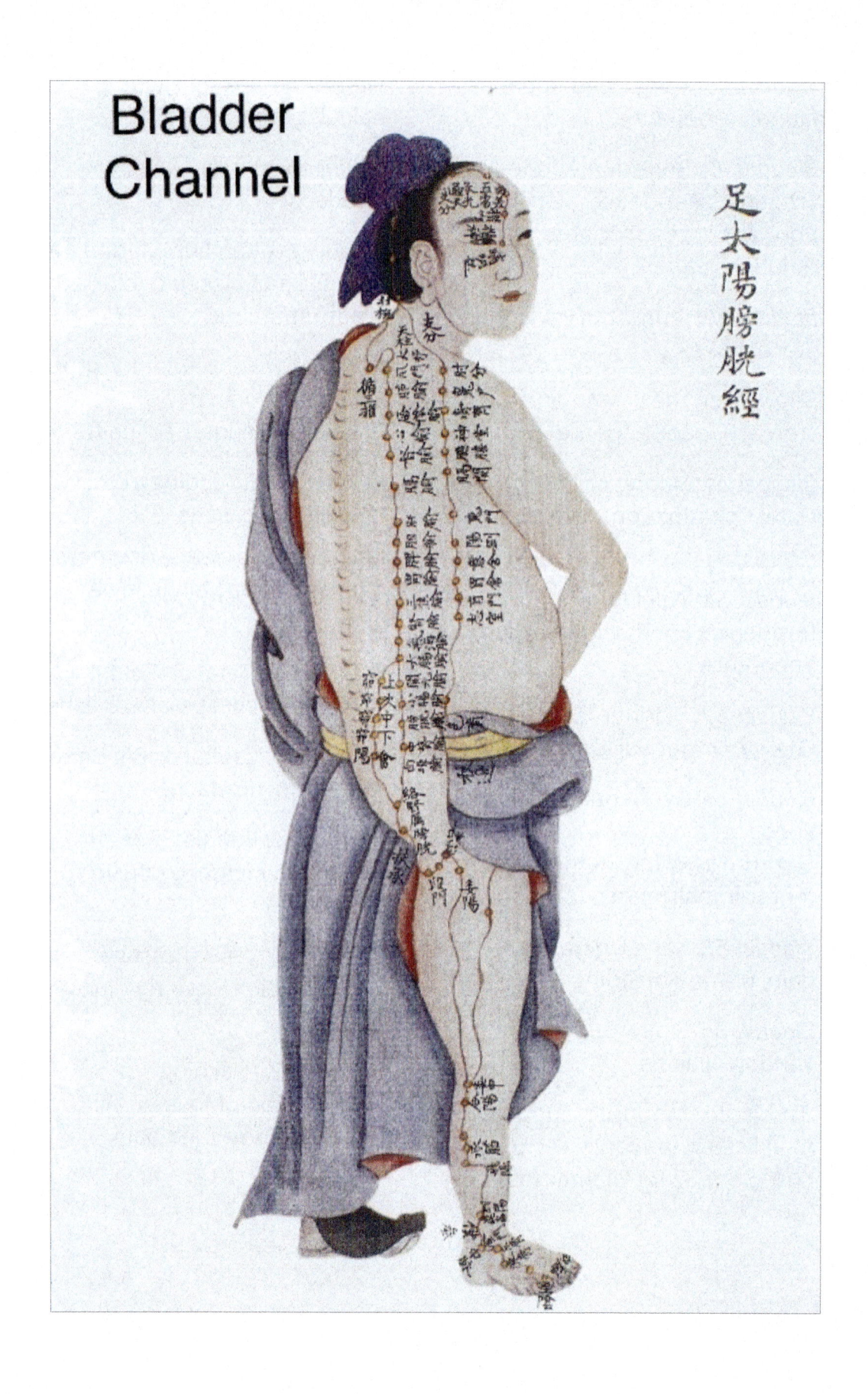

足太陽膀胱經

NOTES

"You do not drown by falling into a river, but staying submerged in it."
Paulo Coelho

KIDNEY POINTS AND USES

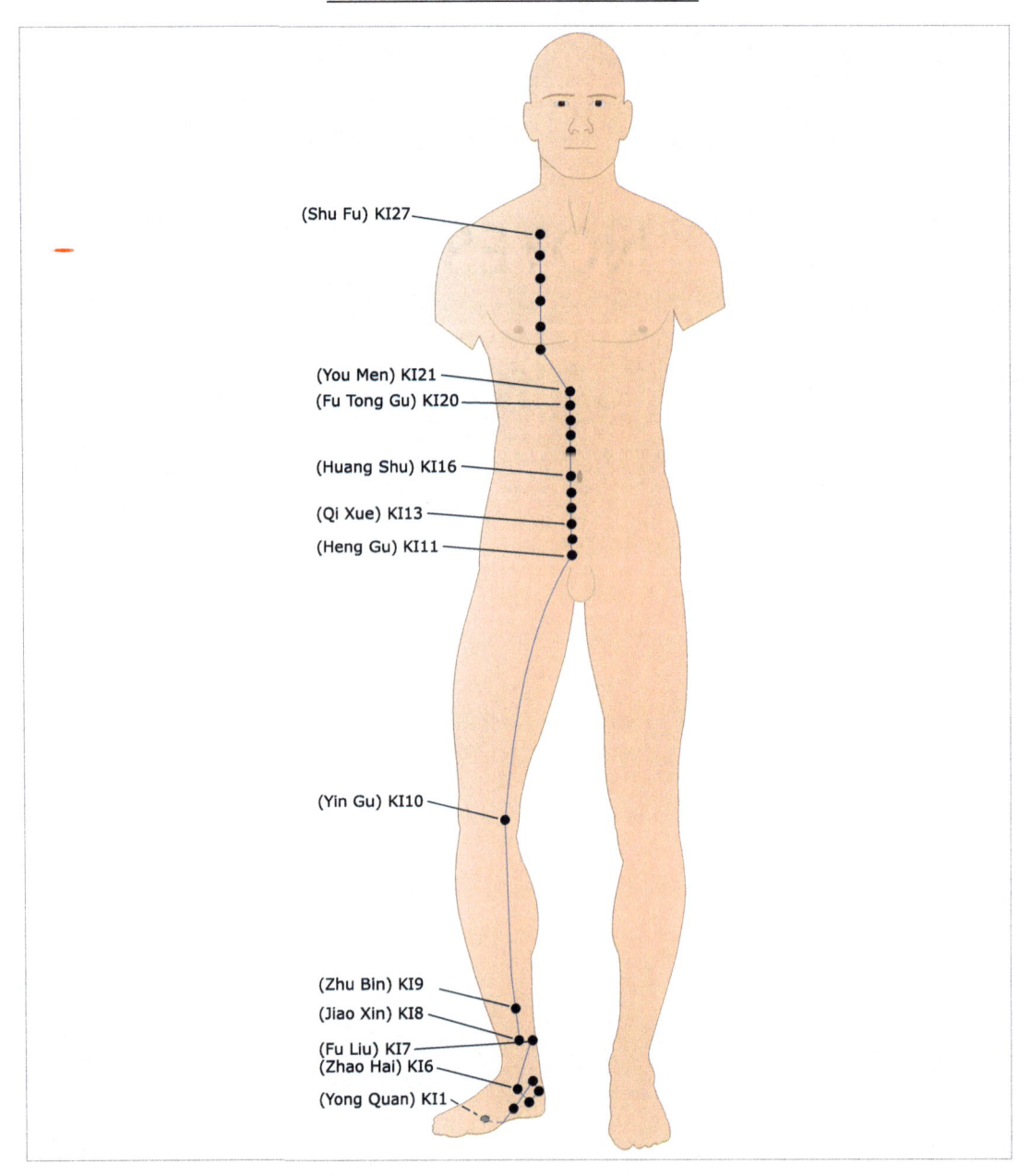

(Shu Fu) KI27
(You Men) KI21
(Fu Tong Gu) KI20
(Huang Shu) KI16
(Qi Xue) KI13
(Heng Gu) KI11
(Yin Gu) KI10
(Zhu Bin) KI9
(Jiao Xin) KI8
(Fu Liu) KI7
(Zhao Hai) KI6
(Yong Quan) KI1

Kidney 1: Gushing Spring This is the only acu-point that touches Mother Earth
Blurred vision, schizophrenia, dizziness

Kidney 2: Blazing Valley, Prolapse uterus

Kidney 3: Great Ravine or Stream, Insomnia, tinnitus, deafness

Kidney 4: Large Goblet or Bell, Heel pain, asthma

Kidney 5: Water Spring, Irregular periods

Kidney 6: Shining Sea, Eye disorders, insomnia

Kidney 7: Recover Flow, Night sweating, fevers, edema

Kidney 8: Intersecting Reach or Coming on Time
Irregular periods, uterine bleeding

Kidney 9: Guest House, Mental illness, hernia pain

Kidney 10: Yin Valley, Knee pain, regulation of Qi

Kidney 11: Pubic Bone, External genital pain, urine retention

Kidney 12: Great Manifestation, Same as 11

Kidney 13: Qi Hole or Source Point, Irregular periods

Kidney 14: Fourfold Fullness, Same as 13, postpartum pain

Kidney 15: Central Flow, Abdominal pain, irregular periods

Kidney 16: Shu of Abdominal Fu, Vomiting, abdominal pain

Kidney 17: Shang Bend or Crook, Same as 16

Kidney 18: Stone Pass, Constipation, fullness of abdomen*Kidney 19:* Yin Metropolis, Same as 18

Kidney 20: Open or Passing Valley, Same as 18, weakness of spleen

Kidney 21: Dark or Secluded Gate, Irritability restlessness, chest pain

Kidney 22: Corridor Walk, Asthma, cough vomiting

Kidney 23: Spirit Seal, Poor appetite, cough, asthma

Kidney 24: Spirit Ruins or Soul's Place
Associated with the heart. Asthma, cough fullness of chest

Kidney 25: Spirit or Mind Storehouse, Chest pain, asthma, cough

Kidney 26: Lively Center, Same as 25

Kidney 27: Shu Mansion
Cough, asthma. One of my instructors said this point was good to tap for energy with both fists, like gorillas beating their chest before a fight.

Kidney channel

Pericardium Points and Uses

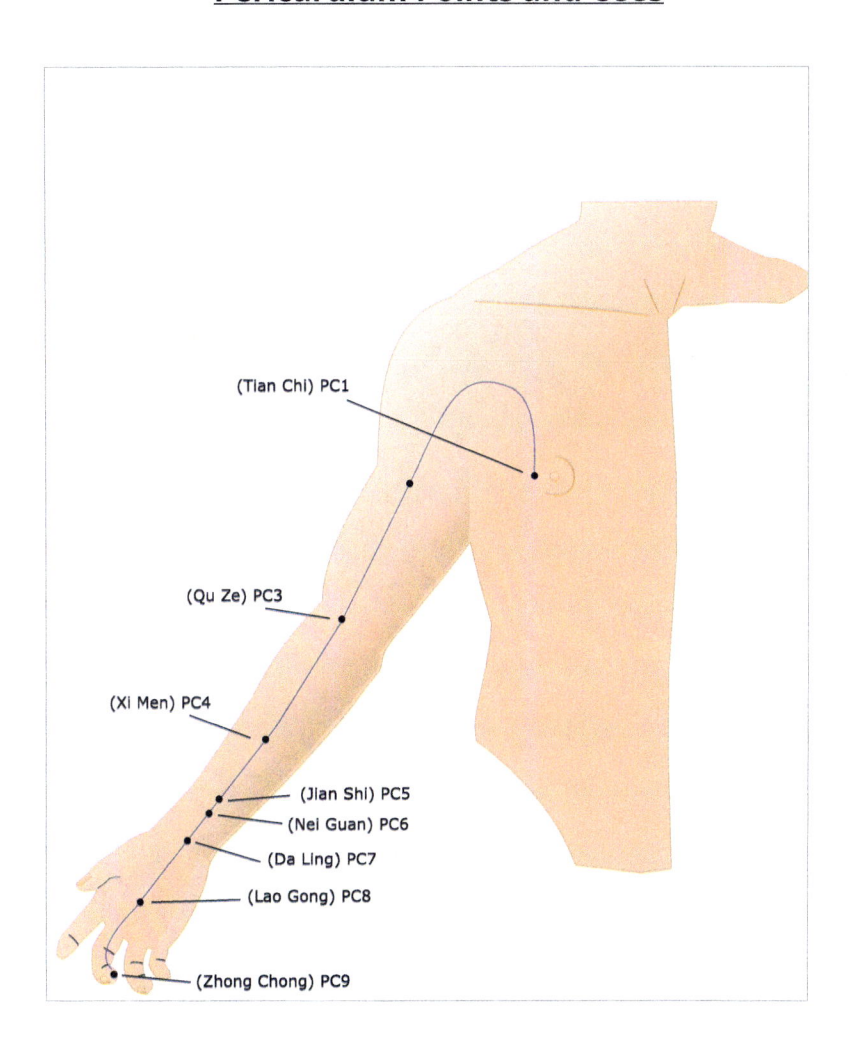

(Tian Chi) PC1
(Qu Ze) PC3
(Xi Men) PC4
(Jian Shi) PC5
(Nei Guan) PC6
(Da Ling) PC7
(Lao Gong) PC8
(Zhong Chong) PC9

Pericardium 1: Celestial Pool or Pond, Full sensation in chest

Pericardium 2: Celestial Spring, Cardiac pain, pain in arm

Pericardium 3: Marsh at the Bend or Curved Pond
Palpations, cardiac pain, vomiting, restlessness, arm pain

Pericardium 4: Xi Gate, Palpations, chest pain

Pericardium 5: Intermediary Courier or Messenger
Angina, palpations hypertension

Pericardium 6: Inner Pass
Morning sickness, dizziness, insomnia, vertigo

Pericardium 7: Great Mound, Palpitations, vomiting

Pericardium 8: Palace of Toil
Cardiac pain, bad breath, mouth ulcers, profuse sweating of the hands

Pericardium 9: Central Hub or Fort

I tell my students an easy way to remember this location is when you get mad and fired up and give the middle finger ;)
Coma, sunstroke, having difficulty speaking, baby that won't stop crying at night

NOTES

"I've experienced several different healing methodologies over the years-counseling, self-help seminars, and i've read a lot-but none of them will work unless you really want to heal."
Lindsay Wagner

San Jiao Points and Uses

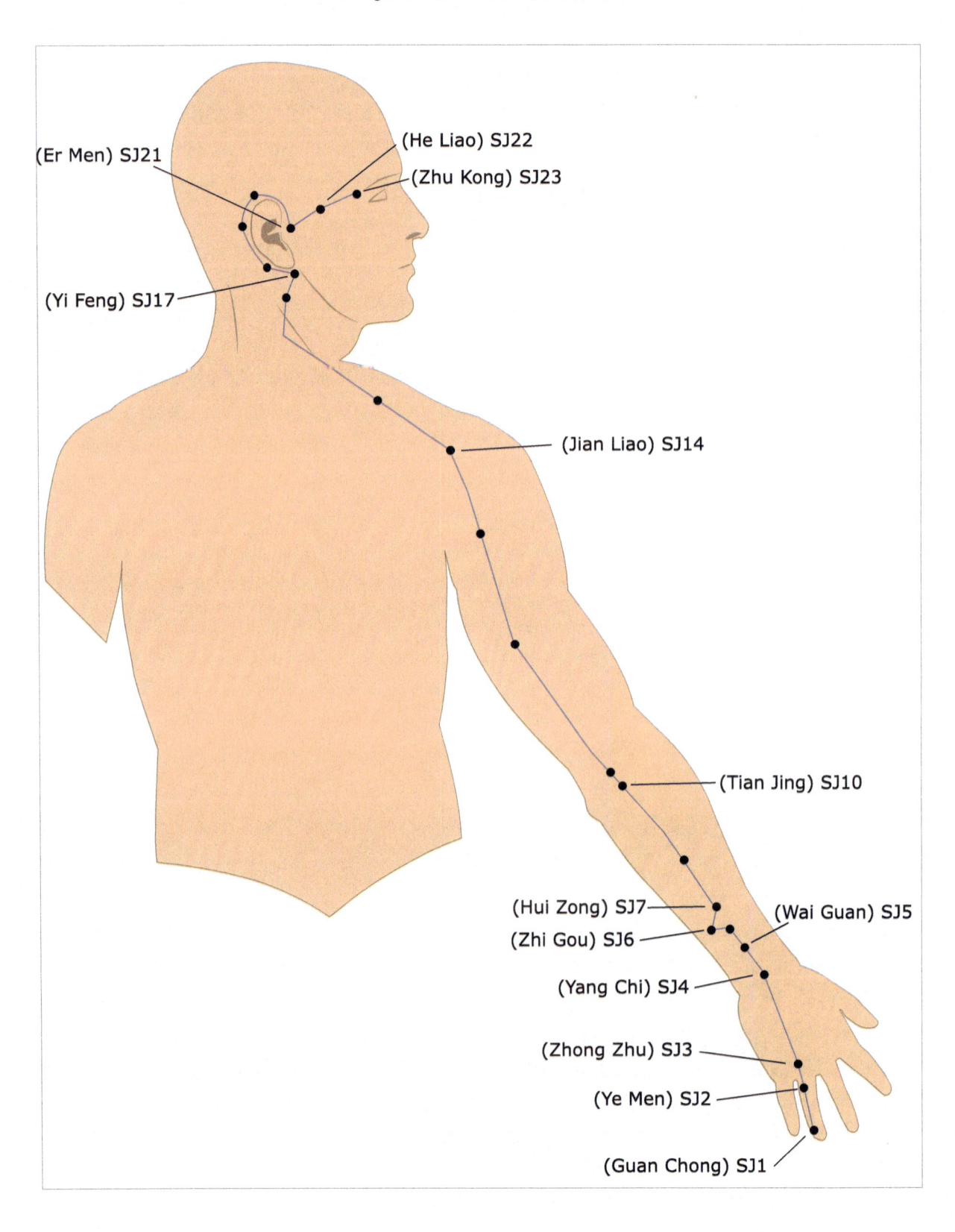

San Jiao 1: Passage Hub or Essential Pass, Sore throat, headache, red eyes

San Jiao 2: Humor or Fluid Gate Blurred vision, headache, sore throat, tinnitus

San Jiao 3: Central Islet Hand numbness, finger motor impairment, tinnitus

San Jiao 4: Yang Pool Thirst due to diabetes, shoulder, wrist, arm pain

San Jiao 5: Outer Pass Pain upper extremities, one sided headache, mumps

San Jiao 6: Branch Ditch, Shoulder, arm pain

San Jiao 7: Convergence and Gathering, Aching arm, epilepsy

San Jiao 8: Three Yang Connection Sudden deafness or hoarseness, pain in upper arm

San Jiao 9: Four Rivers, Sudden hoarseness, forearm pain

San Jiao 10: Celestial Well, Neck, shoulder & arm pain

San Jiao 11: Clear Cold Abyss Headache, toothache, pain in neck

San Jiao 12: Dispersing Riverbed or Relieve Thirst Diabetes, back & shoulder pain

San Jiao 13: Upper Arm Convergence, Shoulder & arm pain

San Jiao 14: Shoulder Bone Hole, Heaviness and pain of arm

San Jiao 15: Celestial Bone Hole, Shoulder and elbow pain

San Jiao 16: Celestial Oriole, Headache, facial swelling

San Jiao 17: Wind Screen Trigeminal neuralgia, facial paralysis, tinnitus

San Jiao 18: Spasm or Convulsion Vessel, Headache, deafness, tinnitus

San Jiao 19: Skull's or Brain Rest, Headache, tinnitus

San Jiao 20: Angle Vertex Cornea cloudiness, swollen gums, tinnitus, stiff neck, dry mouth

San Jiao 21: Harmony Bone Hole or Ear Gate Clicking jaw, tinnitus, cheek pain, toothache

San Jiao 22: Normalizing Hole, Lock Jaw, Head heaviness or headache

San Jiao 23: Silk Bamboo Hole Twitching eyelid, blurred vision, eye pain

San Jiao

手少陽三焦經

NOTES

"There are many ways to heal. Arrogance may have a place in technology but not in healing. I need to get out of my own way if I am to heal."
Anne Wilson Schaef

Gall Bladder Points and Uses

Gall Bladder 1: Pupil Bone Hole, Eye disorders, headache

Gall Bladder 2: Auditory Convergence, Tinnitus, toothache, facial paralysis

Gall Bladder 3: Upper Gate or Hinge, Toothache, headache, dizziness

Gall Bladder 4: Suspended Fullness, Neck pain

Gall Bladder 5: Suspended Skull, Neck pain

Gall Bladder 6: Suspended Tuft, Dizziness, blurred vision

Gall Bladder 7: Temporal Hairline Curve , Same as 6

Gall Bladder 8: Valley Lead, One sided headache

Gall Bladder 9: Celestial Hub, Dizziness, blurred vision, headache, palpations

Gall Bladder 10: Floating White, Deafness, tinnitus, headache

Gall Bladder 11: Head Portal Yin, Dizziness, headache

Gall Bladder 12: Completion Bone Swelling of cheeks, facial paralysis, blurred vision, headache

Gall Bladder 13: Root Spirit, Stiff, pain in neck, headache, blurred vision

Gall Bladder 14: Yang White, Twitching eyelids, blurred vision

Gall Bladder 15: Head Overlooking Tears, Headache

Gall Bladder 16: Eye Window, Headache, glaucoma, blindness

Gall Bladder 17: Upright Construction, Eye pain, toothache

Gall Bladder 18: Spirit Container or Support, Headache, eye pain

Gall Bladder 19: Brain Hollow, Blurred vision, neck and head pain

Gall Bladder 20: Wind Pool or Pond, Common cold, headache, neck pain

Gall Bladder 21: Shoulder Well 20& 21 great for migraines but not if pregnant

Gall Bladder 22: Armpit Abyss, Difficulty lifting the arm

Gall Bladder 23: Sinew Seat, Chest pain, fullness

Gall Bladder 24: Sun and Moon Hiccup, jaundice, acid reflux. It's the Front Mu point of Gall Bladder that connects to Back Shu BL19

Gall Bladder 25: Capital Gate
Chest distention, low back pain. Front Mu point of Kidneys that connects with BL 23

Gall Bladder 26: Girdling Vessel, Irregular periods, abdominal pain

Gall Bladder 27: Fifth Pivot, Leukorrhea, uterine bleeding, lower abdominal pain

Gall Bladder 28: Linking Path, Prolapse uterus

Gall Bladder 29: Squatting Bone Hole, Pain in lower back and limbs, paralysis

Gall Bladder 30: Jumping Round, Knee, shin, low back pain

Gall Bladder 31: Wind Market, Muscular atrophy, motor impairment lower limbs

Gall Bladder 32: Central River, Knee pain and same as 31

Gall Bladder 33: Knee Yang Gate, Pain and swelling of knees

Gall Bladder 34: Yang Mound Spring Master Point for tendons and muscles. Good for pain in the body especially broken ribs. Bitter taste, diseases of liver and gall bladder

Gall Bladder 35: Yang Intersection, Weakness of foot, knee pain

Gall Bladder 36: Outer Hill or Mound, Neck Pain

Gall Bladder 37: Bright Light, Myopia, night blindness, one sided headache

Gall Bladder 38: Yang Assistance, One sided headache, chest pain

Gall Bladder 39: Suspended Bell, Neck, head pain, paralysis lower limbs

Gall Bladder 40: Hill Ruins, Muscular atrophy and paralysis lower limbs

Gall Bladder 41: Foot Overlooking Tears, Eye disorders, painful toes

Gall Bladder 42: Earth Fivefold Convergence
Itchy eyes, swelling breasts, pain and swelling of the dorsal side of foot which is lymphatics and breast in reflexology.

Gall Bladder 43: Pinched Ravine

Blurred vision, dizziness, tinnitus, swelling and pain of breast

Gall Bladder 44: Foot Portal Yin, Tongue rigidity, hiccups, eye diseases

Gall Bladder

LIVER POINTS AND USES

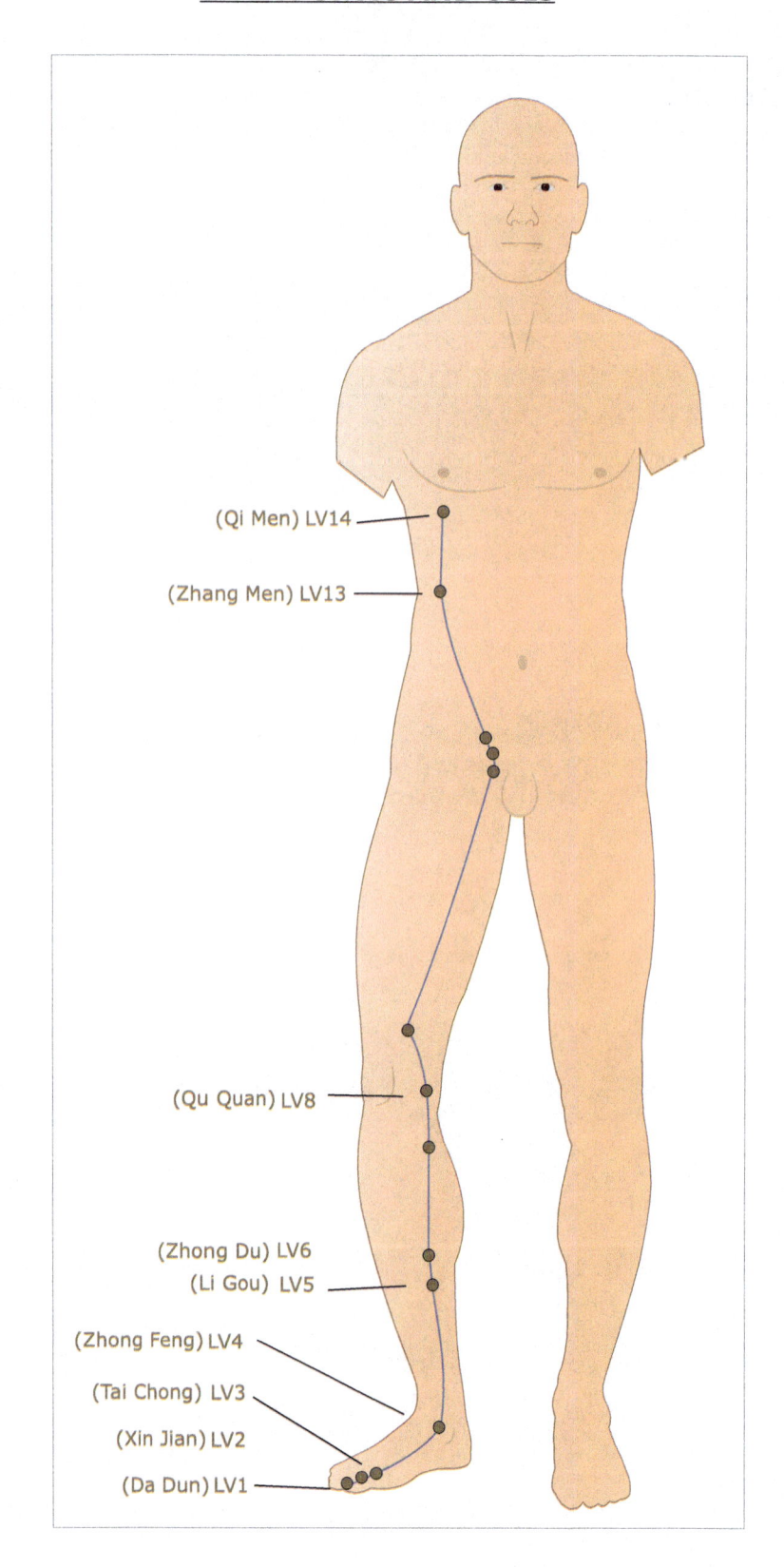

(Qi Men) LV14
(Zhang Men) LV13
(Qu Quan) LV8
(Zhong Du) LV6
(Li Gou) LV5
(Zhong Feng) LV4
(Tai Chong) LV3
(Xin Jian) LV2
(Da Dun) LV1

Liver 1: Large Pile, Prolapse uterus, hernia

Liver 2: Moving Between, Convulsion, eye pain, glaucoma

Liver 3: Great Surge, Dizziness, vertigo. Insomnia, schizophrenia

Liver 4: Mound Central, Pain around belly button, hernia

Liver 5: Woodworm Canal Abdominal pain, diarrhea, profuse leukorrhea

Liver 6: Central Metropolis, Same as 5

Liver 7: Knee Joint, Knee pain, sore throat

Liver 8: Spring at Bend Knee swelling, prolapse uterus, lower abdominal pain

Liver 9: Yin Bladder, Lumbosacral pain, irregular periods

Liver 10: Foot Five Li, General lassitude, urine retention

Liver 11: Yin Corner, Leg and thigh pain, irregular periods

Liver 12: Urgent Pulse

Prolapse uterus, lower abdominal pain, hernia

Liver 13: Camphorwood Gate Hepatitis, vomiting, diarrhea, weak spleen and stomach

Liver 14: Cycle Gate, Acid reflux, soothes liver, chest pain

NOTES

*"What happens when people open their hearts?
They get better"*
Rumi

12 Officials of the Court

HT	King	Source of Shen and clear insight
LU	Minister to King	Receives pure Chi from heaven
LV	General	Sets Strategy
GB	Judge	Decisions of court & wise judgment
PC	Messenger to King	Protects the King
SP	Official	in charge of grainery, transform & transport
ST	Official	in charge of rotting & ripening
LI	Official	in charge of drainage
SI	Receiving Official	separates pure from impure
KI	Minister of Health	strength of body, controls water
SJ	Irrigation Official	balance & harmony, water channels
BL	Minor District Official	controls storage of water & Excretes fluids

In the Yellow Emperor, the 12 major meridians were more like real people, serving the monarch. They each had their jobs to keep the court running smoothly. All depended on the King and the court to maintain good health.

NOTES

"All healing is first a healing of the Heart"
Carl Townsend

JIAOS, TONGUE & FEET

San Jiao has 3 sections. An upper, middle and lower which leads to it being called triple heater, burner or warmer.

Upper represents the chest and the overall function of the heart and lungs in transporting Chi and blood to various parts of the body.

Middle represents the stomach and spleen in digestion and absorption.

Lower Jiao is seen in the kidney and bladder as controlling storage and secretion of urine and water metabolism.

The human body is also divided into three sections. Chinese anatomical position has the arms up in the air as opposite to Western were the arms are lateral by the sides. In Chinese the Upper section is heaven were all the 5 senses are sight, hearing, taste, touch and smell. We receive information, food and Qi. The Middle section (human) is were we process and decide what is useful and what is not. And the Lower section (earth) is where we eliminate what is not needed. That balancing taking place, hence the phrase between heaven and earth.

One can really see what's reflected in the body within the 3 Jiaos on the tongue.

A so called normal tongue is pink in coloring with a nice thin white coat. It should have spirit.

Body	Color & shape	Yin organs, Qi & blood
Coating	Color Thickness	Cold or Hot Excess / Deficiency
Movement/ Spirit	Side to side Quivering Rolled up Rolled down	Wind Heart/spleen Qi Heart heat excess Heart heat deficiency

BODY

Red	Heat
Pale	Cold
Purple	Blood Stasis
Dry	Deficiency

COATING

Thin White	Normal
Thick White	Cold, Wind or Dampness
Yellow	Heat
Greasy or Slippery	Dampness/Phlegm
White & Black	Spleen Dampness
Yellow & Black	Heat in Stomach & Intestines
Black	Kidney Exhaustion

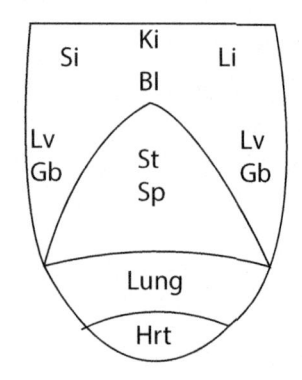

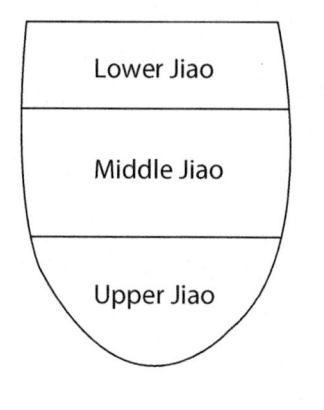

TONGUE ANALYSIS

MORE ON THE BODY

Cracked	Yin Deficiency
Large center crack	Back pain
Red tip with raised taste buds	Insomnia
Deviated	Wind invading could be early warning sign of stroke
Thin shaped	Blood deficiency
Swollen with teeth marks on the side	Spleen Yang Deficiency
Hammer shaped	Stomach, spleen & kidney deficiency
Long	Blazing heart fire
Short	Spleen yang deficiency

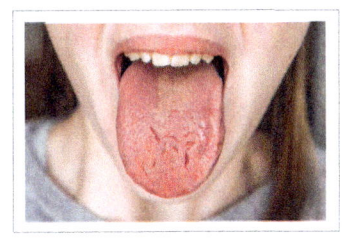

Redness and brown fur in large intestine lower jiao area indicates heat. Cracking in stomach area.

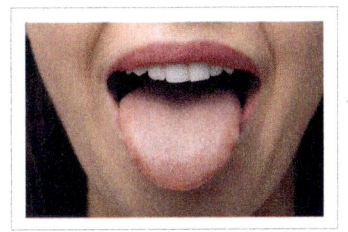

Dampness and spleen deficiency showing in swollen tongue with teeth marks on the side

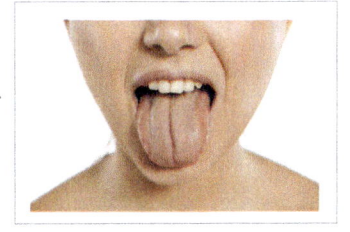

Swollen and teeth marks as before. The long center heart crack indicates a tendency to a heart pattern.

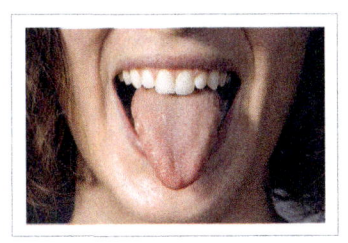

Pointing tongue with red dots indicates insomnia. There's also some dampness swollen area with teeth marks on side.

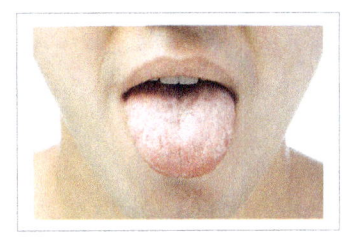

Thick white coating indicating Stomach Qi deficiency

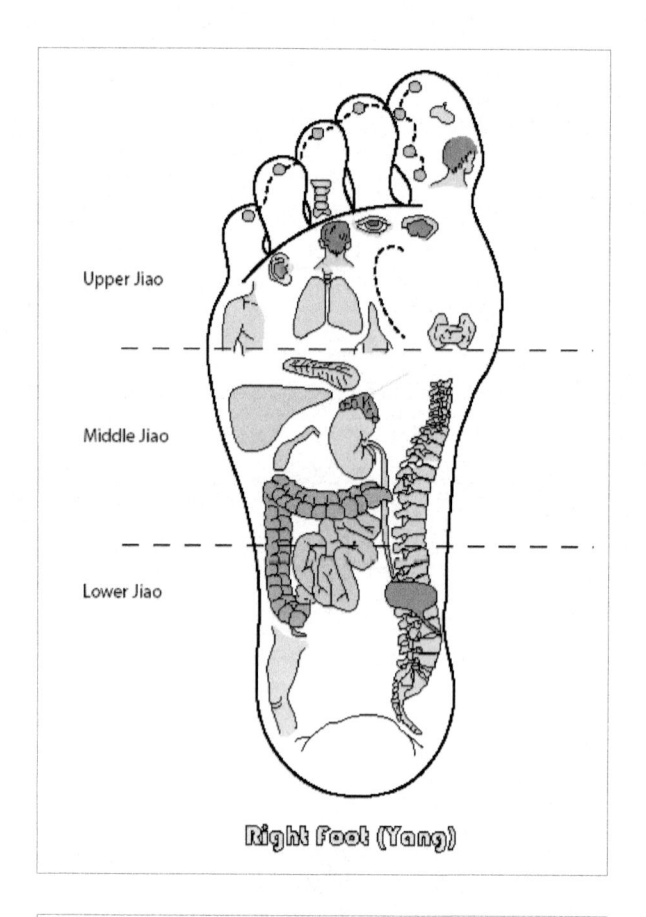

Upper Jiao

Middle Jiao

Lower Jiao

Right Foot (Yang)

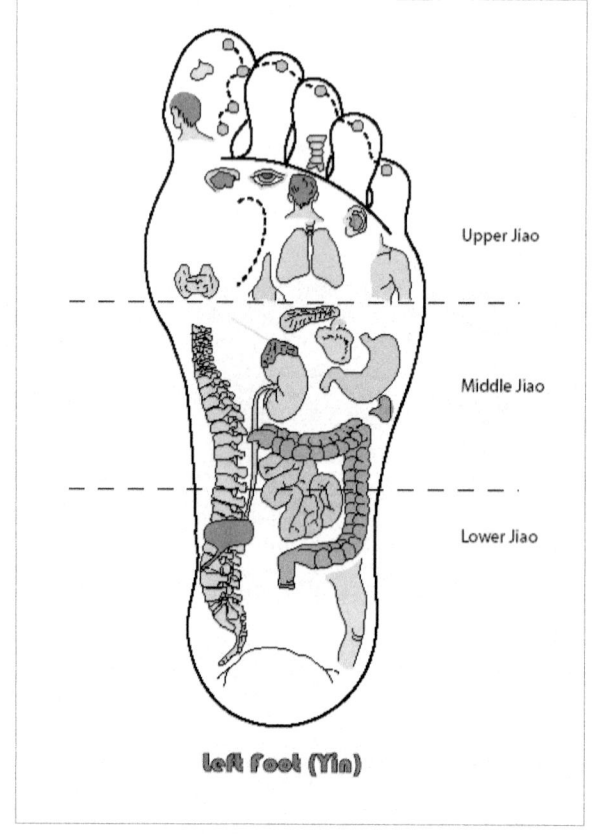

Upper Jiao

Middle Jiao

Lower Jiao

Left Foot (Yin)

PULSES

There are eight categories of pulse types which can be separated into twenty eight qualities.
- Pulses should also have three characteristics:
- Spirit reflects Heart and blood Qi
- Stomach Qi: Stomach is the root of the five yin organs and needs Stomach Qi to reach the Lung meridian
- Root reflects Kidney Qi

The first two are more superficial while the Root is on a deeper level.

Floating	1: Floating Type
Hollow	1: Floating Type
Leather	1: Floating Type
Deep	2: Sunken Type
Firm	2: Sunken Type
Hidden	2: Sunken Type
Slow	3: Slow Type
Knotted	3: Slow Type
Intermittent	3: Slow Type
Rapid	4: Rapid Type
Hasty	4: Rapid Type
Slippery	5: Slippery Type
Moving	5: Slippery Type
Choppy	6: Choppy Type
Empty	7: Deficient Type
Weak-Floating	7: Deficient Type
Minute	7: Deficient Type
Scattered	7: Deficient Type

Weak	7: Deficient Type
Fine	7: Deficient Type
Short	7: Deficient Type
Full	8: Full Type
Over Flowing	8: Full Type
Big	8: Full Type
Wiry	8: Full Type
Tight	8: Full Type
Long	8: Full Type
Slowed Down	If soft with good rhythm & strength indicates good health

Pulse Diagnosis

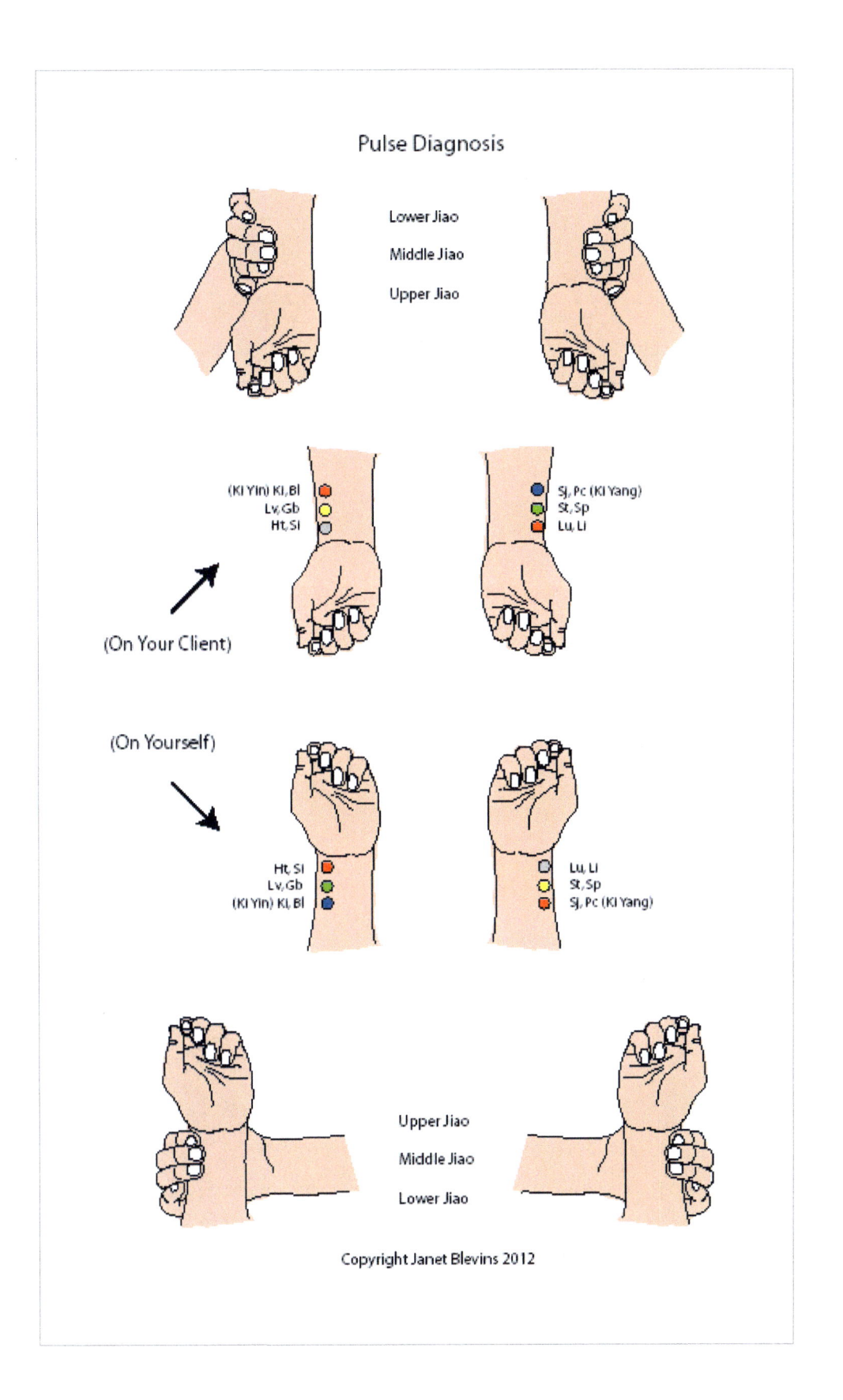

Lower Jiao
Middle Jiao
Upper Jiao

(KI Yin) Ki, Bl
Lv, Gb
Ht, Si

Sj, Pc (KI Yang)
St, Sp
Lu, Li

(On Your Client)

(On Yourself)

Ht, Si
Lv, Gb
(KI Yin) Ki, Bl

Lu, Li
St, Sp
Sj, Pc (KI Yang)

Upper Jiao
Middle Jiao
Lower Jiao

Copyright Janet Blevins 2012

NOTES

"Eventually you come to the understanding that love heals everything, and love is all there is."
Gary Zukan

COMMAND, ALARM AND 5 SHU POINTS

Command points influence the behavior of Qi or activity in that meridian. All command points are located between the finger tips and elbows (Heaven) or tips of the toes and knees (earth) except for one point. That is Stomach Xi-Cleft.

There are also five types of Command points.

- **Luo Points** connect husband (yang) and wife (yin) source points.
- **Tonification Points** improve quality of Qi in that meridian.
- **Sedation Points** slow down the quality of Qi in that meridian.
- **Xi-Cleft Points** cause movement of Qi in a meridian but not tonify or sedating of it.
- **Yuan Source Points** are where the original Qi curriculum is retained.
- **Alarm Points** denote the reflection of the efficiency of a meridian which there is two types.
- **Back Shu Points** are located on the spine and reflect Yang activity.
- **Front Mu Points** are located on the chest and reflect Yin activity.
- **5 Shu Points** normally found on the forearms and legs reflect the level and quantity of Qi.

Ting Well	emerging from a well
Ying Spring	forming a spring
Shu Stream	increasing forming a stream
Jing River	moving to flow like a river
He Sea	entering into the sea

Ting Well energy is small and usually located at the nail bed corners.
Ying Spring is located on palmar and plantar areas.
Shu Strean energy is abundant and is located around wrists and ankles.
Jing River is constant movement between wrist & elbows and ankles & knees.
He Sea is big and deep like an ocean and usually is located near elbows and knees.

Yin	LU	SP	H	K	P	LV
Wood Ting Well	11	1	9	1	9	1
Fire Ying Spring	10	2	8	2	8	2
Earth Shu Stream	9	3	7	3	7	3
Metal Jing River	8	5	4	7	5	4
Water He Sea	5	9	3	10	3	8
Tonify Mother Pt.	9	2	9	7	9	8
Sedate Son Pt.	5	5	7	1	7	2
Luo or Connecting	6	4	5	4	6	5
Xi Cleft or Accumulating	9	8	6	5	4	6
Source	9	3	7	3	7	3
Front Mu Alarm	LU 1	LV 13	Ren 14	GB 25	Ren 17	LV 14
Back Shu Alarm	B 13	B 20	B 15	B 23	B 14	B 18

Yang	LI	ST	SI	B	SJ	GB
Metal Ting Well	1	45	1	67	1	44
Water Ying Spring	2	44	4	66	2	43
Wood Shu Stream	3	43	3	65	3	41
Fire Jing River	5	41	5	60	6	38
Earth He Sea	11	36	8	40	10	34
Tonify Mother Pt	11	41	3	67	3	43
Sedate Son Pt.	2	45	8	65	10	38
Luo or Connecting	6	40	7	58	5	37
Xi Cleft or Accumulating	7	34	6	63	7	36
Source	4	42	4	64	4	40
Front Mu Alarm	ST 25	Ren 12	Ren 4	Ren 3	Ren 5	GB 24
Back Shu Alarm	B 25	B 21	B 27	B 28	B 22	B 19

CUPPING

Cupping is used to remove Cold such as in asthma, arthritis and common cold. The use of glass, bamboo or plastic cups, are used to disperse accumulations of blood such as a bruise. It is also gained popularity in massage to help with tight or spasm muscles. I have also seen it abused, and crazy things for sale to the general public who has no knowledge of how to use them. I start each of my cupping workshops in a show of what not to buy and the first cup I place on a volunteer is what not to do. It gets lots of laughs but is a serious visual way of showing how one can cause damage. Those lines on a plastic pump cup are not goal lines to reach your clients whole body up into.

A vacuum is created drawing the skin and tissue up into the cup. With the glass and bamboo, fire is used. Please do not use this method unless you are trained to do so as injury and burns are a high risk.

There are several types of cupping:
- Static
- Moving (sliding the dragon)
- Flash
- Bleeding
- Needles (acupuncturist)
- Herbal
- Water

Static cupping is placing the cups and leaving them for a length of time. If the suction is light this is tonifying and can be left on the body for up to 30 minutes. A strong suction 5 to 10 minutes.

Moving cups uses less suction without the skin puckering around the edges. A light layer of liniment or oil is place on the skin first so the cups can slide back and forth producing long red sha(shark skin) marks. Both moving and strong suction can leave the client feeling drained. It also leaves varying degrees of bruising.

Bleeding is usually done on DU 14 to remove foul blood. It is also used to decrease a sudden rise in blood pressure, Stagnation, Blood Heat, injuries to help stop stagnation such as swollen ankle and draining pus.

Needles are place in varying acupuncture locations, and then a cup placed over it. The use of moxa can also be used with the needles.
*Only use needles if you are licensed and trained to do so.

Herbal cupping is mostly done using the bamboo cups. The cups are soaked in the herbal solution and placed on the body. If you use a heated solution that was boiled please make sure not to burn your client.

Wet cupping is mostly done using warm water. Great care and skill is required not to make a mess. Warm water fills about 1 to 2/3rds of the cup. I like to use herbal solutions, liniments and/or gemstone or flower essences.

There are marks that come up with cupping. I suggest you search on internet for the different pictures. Marks can fade quickly or last weeks depending on what is going on in the body. Never leave a cup on too long if you see its turning dark. People's diets and medications and heritage effect the discoloring. Blisters can come up if left to long or toxins in the body. If this happens, do not pop or drain the blister.

Discoloration is not a bad thing. It can show stagnation and thus help move it in the body. But again, take a workshop. Also, your client may feel great but they then go home and their partner freaks out with the marks and all kinds of things ensue.

Basic colors:
- Bluish purple cold stagnation
- Purple red damp heat
- Light color mild Qi
- Dark color exuberant Qi

Bamboo cups on left and glass squeeze cups from Germany.

Below a medi cupping set.

Some of my different plastic hand pump cupping sets.

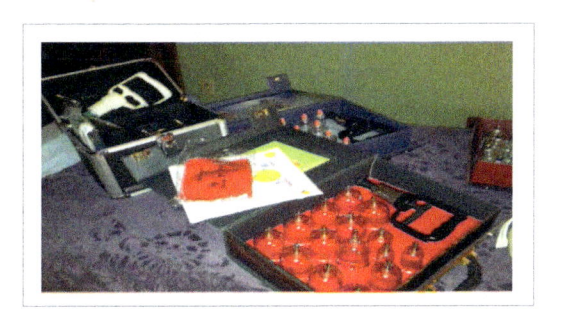

Below various glass cups and how to light one using hemostats with an alcohol soaked piece of cotton ball.

The one on the bottom right is an old bleeding cup.

The placing of hand pump cups on the back for back and shoulder pain.

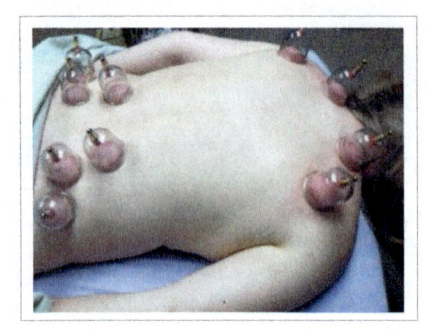

An example of heat that produces steam.

Above an example of placement for low back pain. Place cups along like a belt on low back checking to see discoloration. Do not leave on more than 10-12 minutes unless they get really dark. Then release and move up for another row, moving the energy up to be release downward like a plunger as the back has 4 lines of Bladder channels.

Examples of yin coolness and yang excess with darker colors and of heat in body seen in Darker stagnation marks

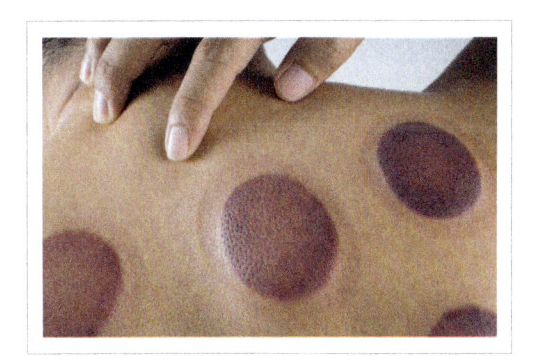

Examples of ashy due to dryness.

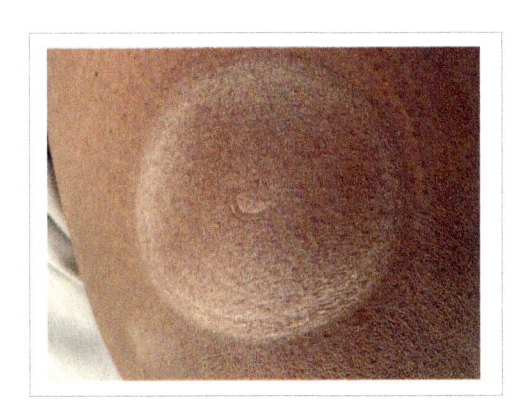

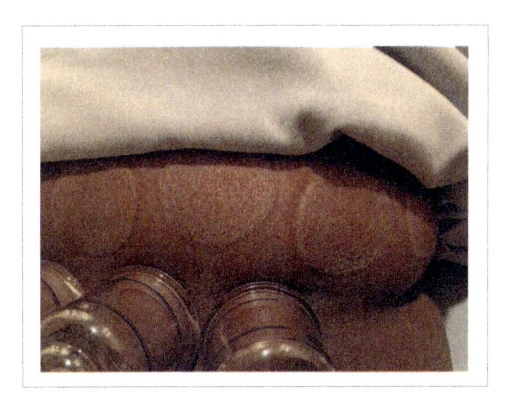

MOXA

Moxa or moxabustion is the act of burning mugwort. It is a strong penetrating Yang energy. It is excellent for Yin cold conditions. Also used for foggy head, stiff joints and melancholy.

Moxa is contraindicated for high blood pressure, skin disorders and heavy menses, along with fever and other Yang conditions. One should also remove moxa once you start to feel it warm up and before it you feel the bite or it could blister and scar.

Artemisia Princeps or Japanese Mugwort is one of the varieties used in moxa. Burnt around Bladder 67 on little toe can turn a breached baby. I have had success with three all turning within 24 hours.

Only use needles if you are licensed to do so.

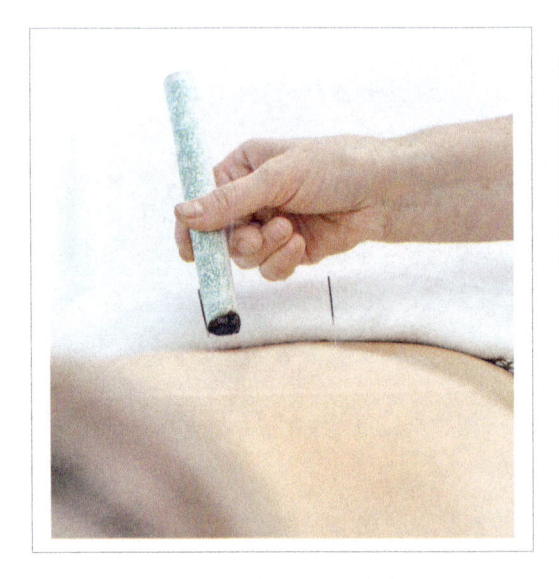

Moxa Points for Hemorrhoids

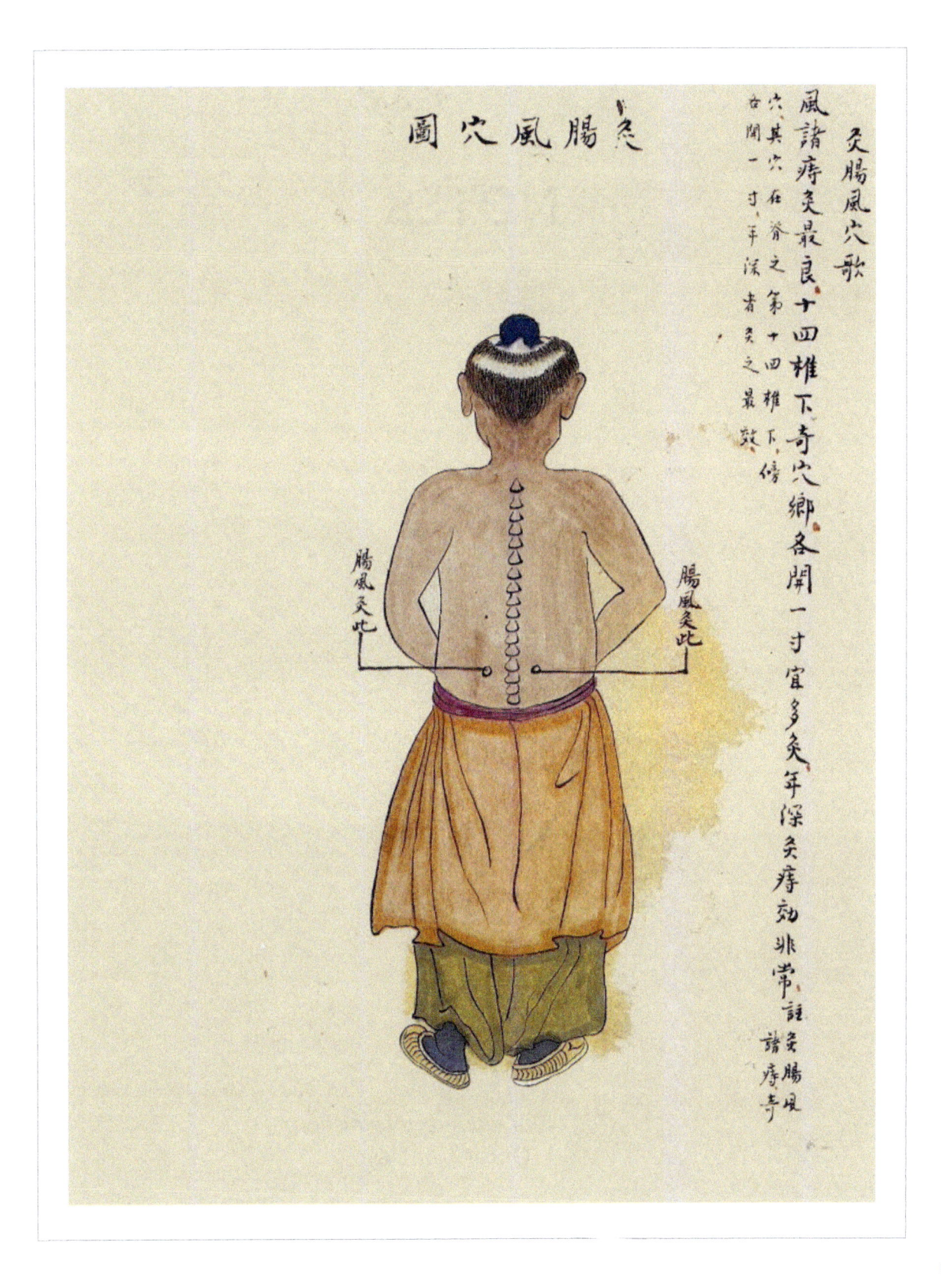

灸腸風穴圖

腸風灸此　　腸風灸此

灸腸風穴歌
風諸痔灸最良，十四椎下奇穴鄉，各開一寸宜多灸，年深灸痔效非常，註灸腸風諸痔等穴，其穴在脊之第十四椎下傍古開一寸，年深者灸之最效

NOTES

"Turn your wounds into wisdom"
Oprah Winfrey

GUA SHA

Gua Sha literally means to scrape. Most commonly used are ceramic Chinese soup spoons, coins or jar lids. Water buffalo horns are also used. Today there are implements you can buy just for the practice. See below:
The wooden mallet and stick is for treating points (Manaka therapy).

Along with the tools you can use liniments or gemstone and/or flower essences. A 30 degree angle is best when applying the scraping friction. Petechiae will then present after a few strokes. These raised red marks is where Sha also gets its name sand or sharkskin, as the raised bumps have that texture.

Do not use around moles, warts or skin tags. Also, do not use on any rashes, burns or wounds. Another contindication is weak, elderly or deficient clients, along with the abdomen of a pregnant client.

The area best used for is pain such as back, shoulder, leg and arm. It is excellent for sciatic and tennis or golfer's elbow. Gua Sha is used along the back intercostals for coughing with a warming liniment to help alleviate stress there.

I have found great success using it on the sternum along with rose quartz essence to open the heart chakra.

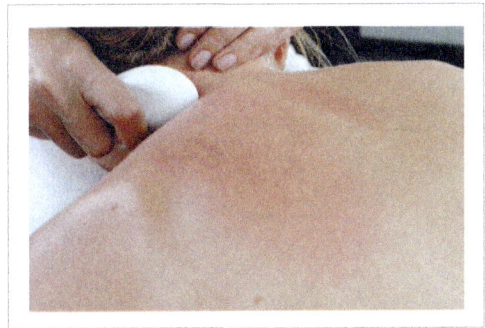

Gua Sha using my favorite tool an Asian soup spoon

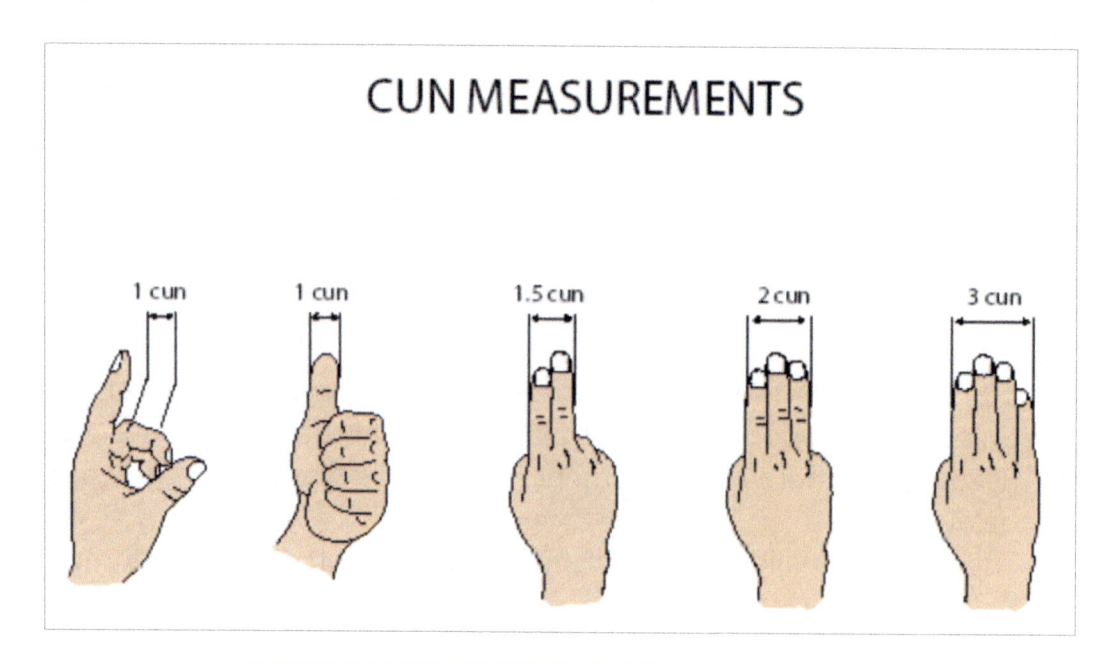

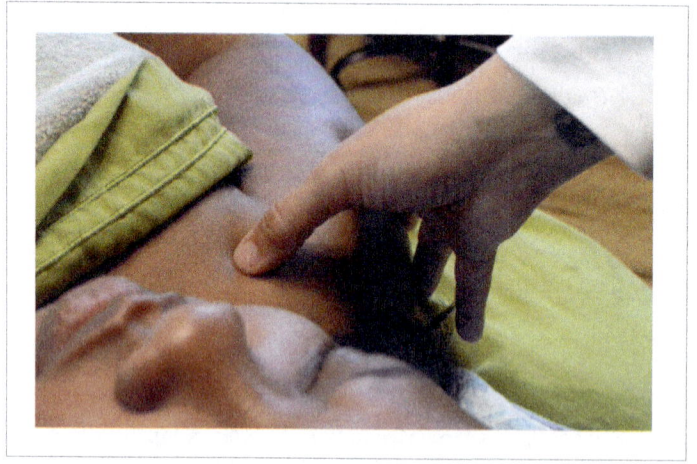

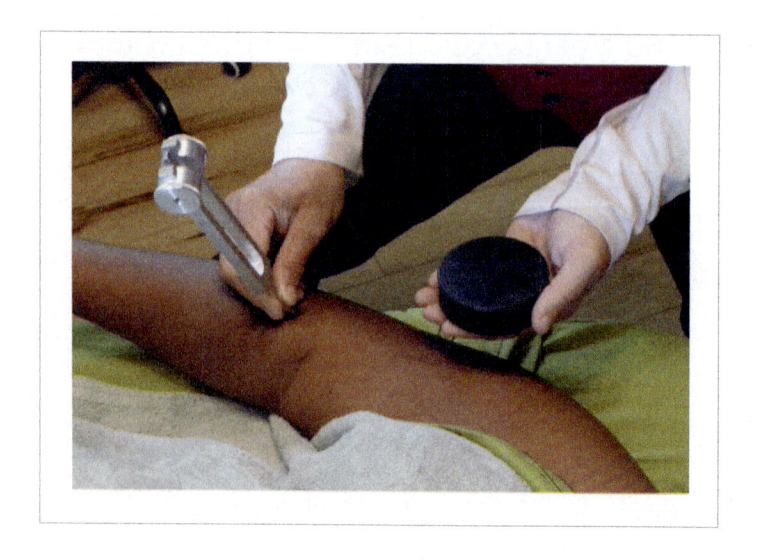

CUN MEASUREMENTS

1 cun   1 cun   1.5 cun   2 cun   3 cun

FINDING POINTS CUN MEASUREMENTS

Measuring units is called Cun to find the location of a point in reference to another point. When applying thumb pressure, it is best to have duck peck thumb which is curved like the bill of a duck to help prevent overuse and damage to one's on thumb.

You can also use tuning forks on some acupressure points. NEVER EVER use tuning forks on neck and head. Weighted forks are placed on the body. Unweighted are used for sound healing. Avoid use with someone with pacemaker.

There are 361 points on the 12 classic meridians and the Governing (DU) and Conception (REN) Vessels.
Lung 11, Large Intestine 20, Stomach 45, Spleen 21, Heart 9, Small Intestine 19, Bladder 67, Kidney 27, Pericardium 9, San Jiao 23, Gall Bladder 44, Liver 14,
DU 28, REN 24

Al most all acu points are natural divots and opening to gather Heaven Qi. Jeffery Yuen (an amazing instructor!) calls them caves. A teacher / shaman in Ecuador Rocio, calls the places Pugyo, places of energy water spirits where things can get stuck and needed cleaning out such a limpia with plants or stones

Not every point is used by bodyworkers. Only a hand full in your toolbox can get you by. Here is some examples:

GB 21, LI 4 & SP 6 are not to be used during pregnancy as they can stimulate premature contractions in the uterus.

Below are a few useful points along with their name.

Headaches:
LI 4 Joining the Valley (Hoku)
GB 20 Gates of Consciousness

Sinus:
ST 3 Facial Beauty
BL 2 Drilling Bamboo

Asthma & Breathing Difficulties:
LU 1 Letting Go
K27 Elegant Mansion
LU 9 Great Abyss

Insomnia:
BL 62 Calm Sleep
KI 6 Joyful Sleep
LV 3 Bigger Rushing

Stomach Ache:
ST 36 Three Mile Point
REN or CV 6 Sea of Energy

Menstrual Cramps:
SP 6 Three Yin Crossing
REN /CV 4 Gate Origin

Plantar Fasciitis:
BL 57 Supporting Mountain
BL 56 Sinew Support
These points along with the heal of the foot, I use cupping with huge success.

Motion Sickness:
PC 6 Inner Gate

Vertigo:
SJ 17 Wind Screen
SI 19 Hearing Palace

Heart attack:
Can be used at onset while calling 911
HT 9 Lesser Surge
SI 1 Lesser Marsh
These are located on the nail bed of the little finger. Bite down hard.

Post Partum:
SP 10: Sea of Blood

Back Pain & Sciatica:
BL 23 Sea of Vitality
BL 47 Door of the Ethereal Soul
BL 48 Womb & Vitals
GB 30 Jumping Round
BL 36 Receiving Support

NOTES

HERBS AND ESSENCESS

With Gemstone and /or Flower Essences, I have been working with the 13 Ghost Points and suggest you try some with your clients.

The 13 Ghost Points was created by Sun Xi Miao who was born in 581 A.D.

The now traditional uses of these points are needled for mental illness such as depression and bi polar.

All disease is first dis-ease in the body. Trauma, guilt, shame, remorse, shock, regret and sorrow are ghosts that can haunt us. I like rose quartz, and lingam along with agrimony, pine or daisy. Please try your own combinations.

If you think of disease/Ghost that knocks on your door, you open it, perhaps even inviting it in. Once you named it "my" fibro, "my" cancer then feed it and share a bed it is harder to remove from your home. Energy attracts like energy. Vibrate on a higher more positive level.

GV / DU 26	Ghost Palace
LU 11	Ghost Convincing
SP 1	Ghost Fortress
PC 7	Ghost Heart
BL 62	Ghost Road
GV/DU 16	Ghost Pillow
ST 6	Ghost Bed

CV/REN 24	Ghost Market
PC 8	Ghost Cave
GV/DU 23	Ghost Hall
CV/REN 1 for females : Yu Men located in the anterior fold of the vagina	Ghost Hidden
LI 11	Ghost Official
Hai Quan located under the tongue in the center of the lingual frenulum	Ghost Seal

Different herbs can be used in a salve to be used with guasha. Tinctures can be added to glass cupping, where a little bit is added to the cup the cup is applied with heat to stay on the body, or just applying to specific acupressure points, dried herb, tincture, salve or infusion.

Note that massage therapist should check their state regulation to see if they are allowed to use fire cupping. Below are just a few suggestions of herbs to place on acupressure points. You can refer back to the list of points in earlier chapter with point number and uses.

Back pain working on Bladder channel I like using any of the following: wild rose, calendula, nettles, rosemary or thyme. If coughing was the cause of back pain, then I also like garlic and mustard. In the case of kidney energy with fear as the root or adrenal fatigue then, calendula, wild rose and rhodiola. Horsetail is also amazing.

Inflammation with pain in joints, I'm a big fan of poke. It is one of my plant allies and guards both corners of my front house growing over 9 feet tall. Yes I know it's poisonous, but nature's poisonous plants have been used for medical purposes for millennia. The berry juice is amazing for inflammation and I am not saying drink it. I actually make a wonderful salve in the fall with bear fat. I call it Poke Beary©.

Sadness, grief, loss working on lung meridian especially 3&4, I like hawthorn, lemon balm, oats, wild rose or geranium.

Headaches peppermint on GB 20,21 and LI4

Insomnia LV 3 lavender, chamomile, hops and passionflower

Anger & resentment LV 3 &GB21 chamomile, lavender, lemon grass, motherwort and agrimony

Anxiety DU 26 located in cleft between nose and lip, H 7, SP 6 clary sage, bergamot, lavender, wild rose.

Blue vervain is great for that fire meridian, bi polar energy out of balance. Also, St. John's wort and valerian.

Calendula for healing from sexual assault. Can also be used for miscarriages.

Dandelion for will power and strength. Also grounding. Great on Kidney

Dizziness use ginger or ginkgo biloba. You can actually fill your belly button with salt but only if you're an inny, then place a slice of fresh ginger and roll a very ting ball of loose moxa on top of the ginger , then light. Best if you have someone to do for you as the lite moxa burns extremely hot and its best if you lie flat and relax. Moving could cause ball to roll off and you get a third degree burn.

Bleeding best to have yarrow fresh or powered. Closes small wounds immediately.

Burns, bites, stings: Plantain, chickweed and mud for the latter two. Echinacea tincture foe snake and spider bites. Aloe vera for burns. Rosewater and lavender mixture sprayed helps reduce pain.

For non herbalist I strongly suggest taking an herbal class or course. I just have some tidbits in here for a hands-on workshop introduction. I am bias and think everyone should take Rosemary Gladstar's The Science and Art of Herbalism
www.scienceandartofherbalism.com

She also has many great reference books. I am fortunate enough to be in the Fire Cider book on page 93 with a, you guessed it a poke recipe. For another wonderful reference, Kat Maier has an outstanding new book Energetic Herbalism, A guide to scared plant traditions integrating elements of Vitalism, Ayurveda, and Chinese Medicine.

And I am encouraging everyone to join United Plant Savers!
www.unitedplantsavers.org

Your contribution will support ongoing conservation and cultivation of at-risk medicinal plants. You can be a voice for the plants.

NOTES

"We cannot direct the wind, but we can adjust the sails."
Dolly Parton

I love Dolly Parton as anyone who knows me can contest to. This is my little altar at work. In feng Shui it is said to place a picture of someone you admire up. I say who better. She gives so much, a true angel on earth. I wanna grow up to be Kind and Generous like Dolly.

RESOURCES

www.lhasaoms.com cupping, moxa, gusha and other supplies
www.healingsounds.com tuning forks
FrenchFrouFrou on Etsy for 18th century Acupoint charts

Herbs and herbal workshops:
www.heartstone-stone.com
www.scienceandartofherbalism.com
www.healingspiritsherbfarm.com
www.woodlandessences.com
www.owlcrafthealingways.com
www.unitedplantsavers.com
www.sacredplanttraditions.com
www.botanicwise.com
www.zackwoodsherbs.com
www.mountainroseherbs.com
www.blazingstarherbalschool.com
www.floridaherbalconference.com
www.internationalherbsymposium.com
www.heartsongfarmwellness.com
www.phyllisdlight.com
www.avenabotanicals.com
www.susanweed.com
www.maryblueherbalist.com
Magazines
https://ahaherb.com
https://herbalgram.org
www.herbquarterly.com
Best herbal allies clothing Etsy.com/shop/TaprootThreads

PRAISE FOR JANET

Janet is incomparable! With her experience, down-to-earth personality and natural gifts, she will positively change your outlook and possibilities with massage and get you out of the box when treating your clients. For those who really want to know and apply the skill set she offers with massage and bodywork, look no further! You will be enlightened and empowered!

Rhonda Barnes, LMBT NC#8270
Owner/Operator Hands on Wellness

Janet Blevins has been a part of our growing and learning process to develop young minds in NC & VA. As a Spa Director, I have relied on her expertise over the past few decades to help me grow my staff and their abilities to provide the top notch technical and spiritual intuition towards their clients on a daily basis. This ability has created the best as we have strived to become The Forbes Best Facilities in the South for the Spa and Resort World. Janet Has been an influential part of this journey and continues to help develop and create this atmosphere for the spa world. She is a true asset to massage and healing techniques towards the future will bring. I met Janet during a continuing Education course on Native American studies and being Native American, realized that I cannot be without her knowledge to help me progress in my career. We have since become life long friends.

Angela Astan Spa Director
www.fearrington.com/spa

Janet Blevins has been practicing acupressure and massage for over 20 years. She is incredibly intuitive with the body and each individual she becomes connected with! Her heart is directly connected to her hands in which she uses her education, experience and sweet being to help heal those who come to her, offering ways each individual to also step into their own self care by incorporating simple acupressure techniques and herbal remedies.

I feel incredibly honored to know Janet and have personally experienced her healing gifts.

Helen Ward   Director of Rosemary Gladstar's The Science and Art of Herbalism
Join www.instagram.com/rosemarygladstar/

Janet Wolf Blevins, is a very gifted Body worker, Herbalist and Teacher, whom I have had the honor of knowing for 30 years. She is always amazing me with her depth of knowledge, her unique way of sharing her understanding of how the body works in a way that is easy to comprehend and has such depth of wisdom gained from her many years of practice. The information provided is very informative and easy to access. Sharing ones gift is the highest form of giving back to humankind.

Andrea Reisen Herbalist
www.healingspiritsherbfarm.com

Janet "Wolf" Blevins is not just a healer, she is that special someone who truly cares, who takes the time to pay attention, to listen and to ask the right questions so one feels seen and heard so the correct course of action can be taken. Blending her gifts of a wise heart, sense of humor, compassion and spiritual path, Janet walks with awareness and kindness and this comes through her writing. You van trust what you read in her new book is shared with knowledge, experience and understanding of the human body, mind, and spirit connection she holds. Janet's words, clear and thoughtful, guide the reader so you feel as if she is right beside you encouraging you along the way.
Kate Gilday Herbalist www.woodlandessences.com

If you have experienced Janet's gifts personally you know she is a master. The Foundation of her written words, the knowledge she has acquired through study and practice are the core and wisdom of this book. For novices and experienced body workers and inquiring minds.

Trishuwa, a spiritual mentor and EARTH-Centered teacher and ceremonialist
www.gaianstudies.org

Janet, thanks for writing my favorite "go to book" for basic Chinese Medicine and Acupressure. I have always loved your classes and teaching methods and this book is like having you in my pocket, for help on my journey. I use it not only as a massage therapist but as a personal guide in daily life, to help me balance stress!

Carolyn B., LMBT

The very first time I met Janet my impression of her forever imprinted in my mind. She is genuine, friendly and willing to help. Her knowledge of massage, the human body and how it all connects is impeccable. Janet is by far the best at what she does. She obtains so much knowledge, but her greatest attribute to me is the way she genuinely loves what she does. Janet is not selfish in sharing her knowledge; she is a teacher and giver at heart.

Latoya Miles

Absolutely Brilliant! Sage Dragonfly is a perfect place, Janet is an excellent instructor. She is warm, accessible, enthusiastic and caring. The classes are fantastic, you feel pushed to learn and try out new techniques with confidence and in a safety environment. Very highly recommended!

Juan Araoz LMBT

Janet is an amazing educator! I have had the pleasure of taking several of her workshops over the last few years and her approach is immersive as well as informative. I found the material immediately useful in my own practice.

Beth Almon, LMBT

I've known Janet since 2004 when we first worked together at a massage therapy school. She was an amazing teacher generous with her time and gifted therapeutic skills. Our friendship has endured over many years. She is my talented massage therapist and my go to continuing education teacher. Her classes are informative, instructive and fun….especially her Ethics classes. She's one of the kindest people I've ever been lucky enough to know. I wish her great success in her next endeavor.

Catherine Koenck, LMBT

I was very fortunate to have met Janet Blevins back in 2004. It was immediately apparent to me that she was someone I would want to follow throughout my massage therapy career. Janet has been teaching classes for Massage Envy's CE program since 2015 and her classes are in high demand. Her wealth of knowledge and ability to educate others is paralleled by few in the massage field making her a elite instructor and mentor. The positive impact she has made on myself and so many other MT's is immeasurable. I will cherish calling Janet my mentor, colleague and most of all my friend!

Justin Smith LMBT #3363 Director of Recruiting and Continuing Education Massage Envy NC

Janet Blevins is a gifted teacher, and this book has proved to be the greatest companion to her work and teachings. Clearly written, packed with information, it is a treasure trove. As a Nurse Practioner, walking with one foot in alternative health world and one in mainstream medicine, her classes and teachings were there for me at the beginning of my journey and her book continues to be a wonderful reference that I dip back into. This is such a much worn textbook upon my shelf and I sincerely hope it becomes one on yours.

Jude Christian
www.integrativeprimarycareva.com

My name is Qiuxia " Lisa" Xu, and currently the owner of Lotus 5 Senses Spa since 2017. I was born and raised in China. I received a Natural Medicine and Nutrition degree from Chinese Medical Association. In US I received my massage therapy license in 2018. Since 2018 all my massage therapy employees and myself have been attending Janet's classes.

www.lotus5sensesspa.com

I have been fortunate to experience the skill and wisdom Janet holds as a healer, teacher, and holder of sacred space on many occasions. She has an incredible capability to translate how energetic patterns show up in the body and spirit. I always come away with a deepen awareness of and in the moment presence with myself after spending time with Janet. I am so excited to be able to have this book to share with my students and to reference myself.
Lucky us!

Suzanna Stone Herbalist www.owlcrafthealingways.com

This straightforward yet comprehensive guide provides the Acupressure essentials for any interested healing arts practitioner. I love how Janet articulates complex concepts with interesting metaphors and stories. She weaves in quotes and anecdotes that make this feel less like a manuscript and more like sitting with her by a warm fireplace as she shares her wisdom. I highly recommend reading this book. Janet has been a source of inspiration to me for almost two decades and I'm excited for her to be able to share her knowledge and lessons beyond the four walls of a classroom and into the hearts and hands of everyone who orders her book.
Ilana Alberico Founder, CEO Spa Space

Janet "Wolf" Blevins, LMBT NC #2835, HHP

Janet has been practicing massage since 1998 and has won Best Massage Therapist in the TRIAD 6 years in a row and maintains a thriving practice. She is a Reiki Master, and has 685 hours massage training certification at GTCC in NC, then traveled to study at Mueller College of Holistic Studies in San Diego, Acupressure certification 734 hours, and 2 Holistic Practitioner degrees one in Western and one in Asian studies consisting of 1000 hours each.

Janet has been Spa Directors, Massage School Executive Director and instructor, massage textbook reviewer and worked at the Olympic Processing Center for the 2000 US Summer Olympic team. She is a National Approved Provider for continuing education #398323-00.

Janet loves books way too much as she has had to replace floor joist in her home, enjoys travel, meeting people and studying indigenous healing and shamanism. Janet is pictured with her acu model man she calls Fred. She does this to educate folks on how Chinese Americans are talked into changing their names to be more acceptable. She first learned this when she worked in the early 90's at a Chinese restaurant in Atlanta. The owner Amy laughed saying "haven't you realized why so many of us are named Amy". Qiuxia who wrote a review early who goes by Lisa. Janet feels your name is important, it has energetic power and encourages everyone to learn to pronounce people's names and learn to say thank you in the language of the country you visit.

www.sagedragonflyworkshops.com for live and online classes and booking a workshop in your area.

Check out my YouTube channel I am not a Masseuse®

Printed in Great Britain
by Amazon